B. P. Pratten

Scotish Songs

Vol. I

B. P. Pratten

Scotish Songs
Vol. I

ISBN/EAN: 9783337191085

Printed in Europe, USA, Canada, Australia, Japan

Cover: Foto ©Thomas Meinert / pixelio.de

More available books at **www.hansebooks.com**

Scotish Songs

IN TWO VOLUMES

VOLUME THE FIRST

Glasgow

HUGH HOPKINS·

1869

EDINBURGH:
PRINTED BY BALLANTYNE AND COMPANY,
PAUL'S WORK.

THE First Edition of "RITSON'S SCOTISH SONGS" was published in 1794, and the number of copies printed does not seem to have been great, as for many years the work has been very scarce. This, and the fact that it is almost the only one of Ritson's works that has not been reprinted, has induced the Publisher to issue this, the Second Edition. While the orthography of the BALLADS has been carefully adhered to, a number of typographical errors in the SONGS have been corrected, and blanks in the MUSIC and GLOSSARY supplied.

J. A.

GLASGOW, MDCCCLXIX.

PREFACE.

—◆—

IT is the observation of an ingenious writer that "the Scottish* melodies contain strong expression of the passions, particularly of the melancholy kind; in which the air often finely corresponds to the subject of the song. Love," says he, "in its various situations of hope, success, disappointment, and despair, is finely expressed in the natural melody of the old Scottish songs." "It were endless," he adds, "to run through the many fine airs expressive of sentiment and passion in the number of our Scottish songs, which, when sung in the genuine natural manner, must affect the heart of every person of feeling, whose taste is not vitiated and seduced by fashion and novelty." For these reasons the words and melody of a Scotish song should be ever inseparable;

* The word *Scottish* is an improper orthography of *Scotish*; *Scotch* is still more corrupt; and *Scots* (as an adjective) a national barbarism: which is observed here once for all, to prevent the imputation of inconsistency and confusion, as a direct quotation should be always literal.

and the editor hopes he will be found to have rendered an acceptable service in the selection he now offers to the public. It may be of some consequence to learn, that this is by no means one of those crude and hasty publications of which there are too frequent instances; it has received the occasional attention of many years, and no opportunity has been neglected of rendering it more worthy of approbation; the editor having even made repeated visits to different parts of Scotland for the purpose of obtaining materials or information upon the subject. How far these pains have been successful, must be left to the candour of the intelligent reader, and to the malice of the *Critical Review*.

The collection is divided into four classes; of which the first will be found to consist of Love Songs, according to the different effects of that pleasing, powerful, capricious, and fatal passion; as courtship, marriage, importunity, complaint, despair, infidelity, absence, constancy, death, and dishonour; the second of Comic Songs, or songs of humour; the third of Historical, Political, and Martial Songs; and the fourth of Romantic and Legendary Songs, or what are usually and properly denominated Ballads.

The orthography of each song is that of the authority from which it is taken, and which (unless, perhaps, in a single instance) has never been intentionally deserted, except where an evident typographical error, or slip of the pen, may have occasioned a correction, of which the reader will be apprised by the usual distinction. This scrupulous adherence to the copies made use of requires that they should be accurately described.

In class 1. songs i., xx., xxvii., xxxiii., xxxv., and lxviii. are taken from the author's Poems, Edinburgh, 1760; songs ii., vi., viii., x., xii., xiii., li., and liii., from the author's Poems, London, 1731; songs iii., iv., v., vii., xi., xxv., xxviii., xxxviii., xliii., xlvii., lv., lix., lx., lxiii., lxv., and lxx., from Ramsay's "Tea-table Miscellany," 1750; songs ix. and xxxvi., from "Roderick Random," London, 1766; songs xiv., xv., xix., xxi., xxii., xxiv., xxvi., xxvii., xl., xli., xlii., xlv., xlvi., xlviii., xlix., l., lii., lvi., lvii., lxi., lxii.,* and lxvi., from "Ancient and Modern Scottish Songs, Heroic Ballads," &c., Edinburgh, 1769 and 1776; songs xvi., liv., lxiv., from the author's Works, London, 1759; song xvii. is from the *Edinburgh Magazine* for December 1773; song xviii., from the author's Works, London, 1762; song xxiii., from a manuscript copy transmitted from Scotland; songs xxix. and lxxi. are from "A Choise Collection of Comic and Serious Scots Poems," Part III., Edinburgh, 1711; compared with and corrected by Ramsay's "Tea-table Miscellany;"† song xxx. is

---

* A different copy of this song, with numerous and considerable variations, is printed in the last edition of "Love and Madness," (1786,) p. 17, for which the author (p. 340) "begs to thank Lady A. L." The alterations do not appear in every instance for the better, and may probably be retracted by the fair and elegant authoress in some future publication, which is one reason why the original stanzas have been preserved; another is that they are already familiar to the public. The editor, indeed, has been assured that the song of "Auld Robin Gray" was well known in Scotland before Lady A. L. was born—a fact which he will certainly believe upon the production of competent evidence.

† *N.B.*—Ramsay neither inserts nor takes any manner of notice of the "second part" of song xxix., which consists of no fewer than thirteen stanzas, but has all the appearance of being by a different and inferior hand.

from "Songs and Fancies," Aberdeen, 1666 ; song xxxi.,
from the authoress's Works, 1751 ; song xxxii., from the
author's Poems, 1756 ; song xxxiv., from the *Gentleman's
Magazine,* vol. xi.; song xxxix., from a single engraved
sheet ; songs xliv., lviii. are from Napier's collection ;
song lxvii. is from a manuscript copy transmitted by Mr
Tytler ; song lxix., from the author's Poems, London,
1781.   In class II. songs i., iii., iv., v., vii., ix., xiii., xiv.,
xviii., xix., xxvi., xxxi., xxxvi., xxxvii., xxxviii., and xl.
are from the "Tea-table Miscellany ;" song ii., vi., xi.,
xv., xxi., xxii., xxiii., xxx., and xxxv., from the "Ancient
and Modern Scottish Songs," &c., 1769 and 1776 ; songs
viii. and xxxii., from Johnson's "Scots Musical Museum ;"
songs xii., xxix., and xxxiii.,* from the Hyndford manuscript, (Bannatyne's collection,) in the Advocates' Library, Edinburgh ; songs x., xvii., xxiv., xxv., xxviii., from
common collections of which the names have not been
preserved ; song xx. is from a manuscript of Charles I.'s
time in the British Museum, (Bib. Sloan. 1489 ;) songs
xxvii. and xxxix. are from the author's songs at the end
of his "Fortunate Shepherdess," Aberdeen, 1768 ; song
xxxiv. is from the "Songs and Fancies," Aberdeen, 1666 ;
and song xli., from an engraved sheet.   In class III.
songs i., vi., viii., xi., xv., xvi., xviii., xix., xxxiii., xxxv. are
taken from the "Ancient and Modern Scottish Songs,"
&c., 1769 and 1776 ; songs ii. and vii., from Dr Percy's
"Reliques of Ancient English Poetry," 1775 ; song iii. is
taken from the "Evergreen," Edinburgh, 1724 ; song

---

* These three songs were originally printed from Lord Hailes's
publication, which turning out, upon a collation with the MS., far
from accurate, the leaves were cancelled.

iv., from "Old Ballads," (published by T. Evans,) London, 1777; song v., from the first edition, Glasgow, 1755; songs ix. and xxxvii., from the "Tea-table Miscellany;" song x., from a manuscript copy, collated with a common stall print; songs xii., xxii., xxvi., xxxi., xxxii. are from Johnson's "Scots Musical Museum;" song xiii. is from a MS. in the Harleian Library, in the Museum, (No. 7332;) songs xiv. and xxx.,* from common collections; song xvii. is from a modern stall copy; songs xxi., xxvii., xxviii., xxix., and xxxiv. are from a collection of "Loyal Songs," &c., 1750; song xxiii. is from a manuscript copy, as dictated to the editor many years ago by a young gentleman, who had it from his grandfather; song xxiv., from the "True Loyalist; or, Chevalier's Favourite," 1779; song xxvi., from the author's Poems, 1749; song xxxvi., from Napier's Collection; song xxxviii., from the author's Poems, Edinburgh, 1786; and song xxxix., from the author's Works, 1762. In class IV. songs i.,† iii., v., and xiii. are from the "Reliques of

---

* This song is sometimes entitled "Lewis Gordon," and said to go to the tune of "Tarry Woo," from which the present air may perhaps have been altered.

† This old ballad, Dr Percy tells us, is given by him from a copy in his folio manuscript, some breaches and defects in which, he says, rendered the insertion of a few supplemental stanzas necessary. These he hopes the reader will pardon, though he does not condescend to inform him which they are. The seeming genuineness and real merit of the ballad, which has all the appearance of being a Scotish production, has prevailed upon the editor to insert it, though from a designedly interpolated copy. The principal incident in the story, whencesoever it came, was well known long before the publication of the "Reliques," and is, in fact, of great antiquity.

Ancient English Poetry ;" songs ii., vi., ix., xi., and xiii., from the "Ancient and Modern Scottish Songs," &c., 1769 or 1776 ; song iv. is from the " Evergreen," Edinburgh, 1724 ; song vii., from a stall copy ; songs viii., xiv., xv., and xvi. are from the "Tea-table Miscellany ;" song x. is from the first edition, Glasgow, 1755, 4to ; and song xvii., from the author's Works, 1759. With respect to the few additional songs, the first is from Ramsay's "Tea-table Miscellany ;" the seven following are from the fourth volume of Johnson's "Scots Musical Museum," (which did not appear till the work was printed off ;) and the eighth is from "Nine Canzonets," &c. By a Lady.

The music, which does not require, nor perhaps admit, of a strict adherence to any particular copy, has been supplied by Thomson's " Orpheus Caledonius ;"* the music for Ramsay's collection, published by himself ; Oswald's " Caledonian Pocket Companion ;" M'Gibbon, Corri, and Napier's collections of Scots tunes, and Johnson's "Scots Musical Museum ;" by other musical publications, and by single songs.† Where a song is either known or presumed to have a tune, which it has been found impossible to procure, blank lines are left for its after insertion with the pen ; and a few songs in the first class are indebted for original airs to the harmonious

---

* It is the second edition of this work which has been made use of, even for the tunes contained in the first, as there is considerable difference in some of the sets.

† There is a MS. collection of (chiefly) Scotish tunes in the library of the Society of the Antiquaries of Scotland, made about fifty years ago for the laird of Macfarlane, but it seems to contain few tunes not to be found in Oswald's or other collections. At least, for a long list of desiderata, it only afforded one single air.

muse of the equally eminent and amiable Shield, whose taste and science have been occasionally exerted in restoring or preserving the genuine simplicity of a corrupted melody, and of whose friendship the editor is happy to boast this testimony.

Some of these tunes no doubt will be found very different from, and perhaps much inferior to, the common or favourite sets; but it may be depended upon that they are immediately taken from the oldest or best authorities that could be met with, and consequently are most likely to be the genuine and original airs; so far, at least, as musical notation can be relied on.

The bass part, which seems to be considered as indispensable in modern musical publications, would have been altogether improper in these volumes; the Scotish tunes are pure melody, which is not unfrequently injured by the basses which have been set to them by strangers: the only kind of harmony known to the original composers consisting perhaps in the unisonant drone of the bagpipe.

All that can be said on the glossary is that the words are more numerous, and the explanations less equivocal than in any former attempt of this nature. The reader may compare it, if he chooses, with that to the "Teatable Miscellany," or collection of "Ancient Scots Songs," &c.; the latter of which, it may be observed, abounds with words not to be found in the work itself.

It may be naturally supposed that a publication of this nature would have been rendered more perfect by a native of North Britain. Without discussing this question, the editor has only to observe that diligent inquiry, extensive reading, and unwearied assiduity, added to the strictest integrity, and most disinterested views, have possibly tended to lessen the disadvantages of an English birth ; and that he is persuaded the present collection, such as it is, will not suffer by comparison with anything of the kind hitherto published in either country.

The following observations, by a late ingenious writer, already quoted, have been thought too pertinent and valuable to be either omitted or abridged :—

" As the Scottish songs are the flights of genius, devoid of art, they bid defiance to artificial graces and affected cadences. A Scots song can only be sung in taste by a Scottish voice. To a sweet, liquid, flowing voice, capable of swelling a note from the softest to the fullest tone, and what the Italians call a *voce di petto*, must be joined sensibility and feeling, and a perfect understanding of the subject and words of the song, so as to know the significant word on which to swell or soften the tone, and lay the force of the note. From a want of knowledge of the language, it generally happens that, to most of the foreign masters, our melodies at first must seem wild and uncouth ; for which reason, in their performance they generally fall short of our expectation. We sometimes, however, find a foreign master, who, with a genius for the pathetic, and a knowledge of the subject and words, has afforded very high pleasure in a Scottish song. Who could hear with insensibility, or without being moved in the greatest degree, Tenducci sing, ' I'll never leave thee ;' or ' The braes of Ballen-

dine;' or 'Will ye go to the ewe-bughts, Marion?' sung
by Signora Corri?

"It is common defect in some who pretend to sing,
to affect to smother the words, by not articulating them,
so as we scarce can find out either the subject or language of their song. This is always a sign of want of
feeling, and the mark of a bad singer; particularly of
Scottish songs, where there is generally so intimate a
correspondence between their air and subject. Indeed,
there can be no good vocal music without it.

"The proper accompaniment of a Scottish song is a
plain, thin, dropping bass, on the harpischord or guitar.
The fine breathings, those heartfelt touches which genius
alone can express in our songs, are lost in a noisy accompaniment of instruments. The full chords of a
thorough bass should be used sparingly, and with judgment, not to overpower, but to support and raise the
voice at proper pauses.

"Where, with a fine voice, is joined some skill and
execution on either of those instruments, the air, by way
of symphony, or introduction to the song, should always
be first played over, and at the close of every stanza
the last part of the air should be repeated, as a relief for
the voice, which it gracefully sets off. In this symphonic
part, the performer may show his taste and fancy on the
instrument, by varying it *ad libitum*.

"A Scottish song admits of no cadence; I mean by
this, no fanciful or capricious descant upon the close of
the tune. There is one embellishment, however, which
a fine singer may easily acquire; that is, an easy shake.

This, while the organs are flexible in a young voice, may, with practice, be easily attained.

" A Scottish song, thus performed, is among the highest of entertainments to a musical genius. But is this genius to be acquired either in the performer or hearer? It cannot. Genius in music, as in poetry, is the gift of heaven. It is born with us; it is not to be learned.

" An artist on the violin may display the magic of his fingers, in running from the top to the bottom of the finger-board in various intricate *capriccios*, which, at most, will only excite surprise; while a very middling performer, of taste and feeling, in a subject that admits of the pathos, will touch the heart in its finest sensations. The finest of the Italian composers, and many of their singers, possess this to an amazing degree. The opera airs of these great masters, Pergolese, Jomelli, Galuppi, Perez, and many others of the present age, are astonishingly pathetic and moving. Genius, however, and feeling are not confined to country or climate. A maid, at her spinning-wheel, who knew not a note in music, with a sweet voice, and the force of a native genius, has oft drawn tears to my eyes. That gift of heaven, in short, is not to be defined: it can only be felt." *

* " Dissertation on the Scottish Music," by William Tytler, Esq.

A HISTORICAL ESSAY ON SCOTISH SONG.

——————◆——————

I. THE most ancient inhabitants of the north parts of Britain, now called Scotland, of whom there is any account, were the Caledonians; a people of the same race with the Britons, or inhabitants of the south parts; children, in a word, of that immense family of Celts, which, pouring out of Gaul, the country, it is supposed, of their original settlement, seems at one time not only to have covered great part of Europe, but even to have overrun the fertile and civilised provinces of Asia.* Their lan-

* A history of the Celts by a person of learning and industry is much wanted. All the French writers who have hitherto attempted such a work (viz., Pezron, Peloutier, &c.) have confounded them with the Goths or Germans; perfectly distinct people. A good foundation, however, has been laid by Schoepflin in his " Vindiciæ Celticæ, Argen," (1754. 4to.) Though the most ancient historians know of no inhabitants in Gaul before the Celts, nor of any Celts but such as inhabited or issued from that country, in which sense only they are called aborigines, it is nevertheless sufficiently pro-

guage, varied by dialect, and corrupted by the influx of
foreign words, is still spoken in Wales, in Ireland, in
the Highlands or mountainous parts of Scotland, in the
Hebrides or Western Isles, in the Isle of Man, in Ar-
morica or Basse-Bretagne, and among the Waldenses, a
little nation in the Alps; and was, two or three centuries ago, the vulgar speech of Cornwall and Galloway,
where, if yet extinct, it continued to be known within
the memory of persons now living. Great part of the
country, however, was, about the time of its invasion by
the Romans, under Agricola, inhabited by a people
called Picts, or Pehts, who are by some thought to have
come from Scandinavia, (the Scythia of Bede,) and to
have driven the more ancient inhabitants out of those
parts (probably all along the north and east coasts) in
which they thought fit to settle; but, let them come
from where they would, they were still a Celtic colony,
and spoke a dialect at least of the language of the
original inhabitants ;* with whom it is highly probable

bable that other countries had been peopled by the same race.
History, in this case, is a child of yesterday.

* For this fact we have the express testimony of Bede, who
observes that a town in Scotland, at the east end of the Picts' wall,
was in their language called *Peanfabel;* and Nennius adds that its
name in the British tongue was *Penzaaul;* as nearly the same word
as the slightest difference of dialect or corruption of orthography
will allow, each meaning the head of the wall; from *pen,* head, and
vallum, wall; which latter word both Picts and Britons had adopted
from the Romans, either from having no synonymous word in their
own language, or none at least applicable to a fortification of that
nature. The Saxons, by adding a usual termination, called it *Pen-
neltun*—i.e., *Pen-vael-tun,* the town at the head of the wall. It
appears from the same Nennius that the Scots (or Irish) called this
place *Cenail*—i.e., *Cean-val*—a name of the same signification, and

they were, in the course of time, indistinguishably blended.

About the middle of the third century a third Celtic

which it has preserved, with a very slight variance, to this day. It is the village of Kinnel, about two miles from Abercorn. (See Innes's "Critical Essay on the Ancient Inhabitants of Scotland," i., 23.) It is needless to add that *pen* and *ceau* mean *head* in the Welsh and Irish languages at this moment. This point is further confirmed by the names of the Pictish sovereigns, which have no resemblance to those in any Gothic list, and of which some are manifestly Celtic, as Ungust, Elpin, Canul, Kenneth, Uven, &c. &c. The names, not only of mountains and rivers, but what is much more to the purpose, of cities, towns, villages, castles, and houses, are, with a very few exceptions, universally Celtic. (See Camden's "Britannia," cxii., (1695;) Innes's "Essay," i., 72, &c., 147; Macpherson's "Critical Dissertations on the Ancient Caledonians," p. 55; the table of parishes in Keith's "Catalogue of the Bishops," and the large "Map of Scotland," *passim;* see also Buchanan's "History of Scotland," vol. i., p. 55, 80, (English translation;) and Malcolme's "Essay on the Antiquities of Great Britain and Ireland, (a Letter to Archimedes the Old Caledonian,") p. 9.) No other vestige of the Pictish language is to be met with; for though Mr Evans suspects the "Gododin" of Aneurin, a celebrated bard of the sixth century, to be in that tongue, ("Dis. de Bardis," p. 67,) and Mr Lhwyd had before expressed the same suspicion with respect to a MS. in the public library at Cambridge, (see Rowland's "Mona Antiqua Restaurata," p. 311; "Archæologia," p. 226,) it seems much more likely that both these articles are in the dialect of the Cumbrian, or Strat Cluyd Britons, according to Mr Lhwyd's other conjecture as to the latter. This very learned and judicious person, who was peculiarly well skilled in the different dialects of the Celtic tongue, agreed with Camden and others that the Picts were of that race. (See the translation of his Welsh Preface in Bishop Nicolson's "Irish Historical Library," p. 104. 1736.) That the men of Galloway were Picts there is indisputable evidence. Ralph, Archbishop of Canterbury, in a letter to Pope Calixtus about the year 1122, calls the Bishop of Galloway the Bishop of the Picts. Joceline the monk, in his life of St

colony arrived in Caledonia, or Pictland: this was a
body of Scots, or Irish, (Scotia and Hibernia being at
that period synonymous,) who landed in Argyle, and

Mungo, *alias* Kentigern, calls it the country of the Picts, (Innes's
" Essay," i., 161;) and Richard, Prior of Hexham, in his account of
the Battle of the Standard, 1138, mentions the Picts no less than
nine different times, calling them " Picti qui vulgo Galweyenses
dicuntur," (Innes's " X. Scrip." i., 158.)   These Galloway men continued to speak the Celtic language till within the present century,
which they would scarcely have done had it not been their primi-
tive tongue. (See Irvine's "Historiæ Scotiæ Nomenclatura," p. 247;
Innes's "Essay," i., 39.)   This province was formerly of great ex-
tent, including, beside the country now so called, Carrick, Kyle,
Cunningham, and Renfrew, and perhaps a part of Clydesdale,
(Innes, i., 160.)   It had its own feudal princes and peculiar cus-
toms, and its inhabitants are usually distinguished, in ancient char-
ters of the Scotish kings, from their other subjects by the titles of
Galwejenses, or *Galovidienses*. (See Innes's " Essay," i. 38, 162, 164;
Crawfurd's " History of the Stewarts," 2.)   These Picts, or Galwe-
gians, claimed the right of making the onset at the Battle of the
Standard as their due by ancient custom.   They were a turbulent,
rebellious, and barbarous people, and the " wild Scot of Galloway"
became proverbial. (See Ross's " Fortunate Shepherdess," (a curious
poem,) p. 51, 87.)   The old inhabitants of the province of Murray
seem also to have been entirely Picts, being so very unruly as to
oblige one of the Scotish kings to disperse them in other parts,
and plant the country with more tractable subjects, about the year
1160, (Innes, i. 159.)   The vulgar language of this province is called
by its historian, Mr Shaw, "the broad Scottish or Buchan dialect,
which," says he, "is manifestly the Pictish."   That the Celtic,
however, has been manifestly spoken throughout this province, as
well as in Buchan and other parts of the east coast, is clear from
the peculiar pronunciation of the present inhabitants, who, like the
Highlanders, use *f* instead of *wh*, as *fa*, *fan*, *fat*, for *who*, *when*,
what, and the like—an infallible symptom of a Celtic foundation.
The Gaelic, indeed, is now spoken in Aberdeenshire, which is on
the same coast, (Macpherson's " Dissertations," p. 62.) The Buchan
dialect, therefore, as extant in a few poems which have been pub-

driving the inhabitants out of that and the adjacent country, held possession thereof for some time. But having been expelled, it would seem, by the north Britons or Picts, they returned with great force, about the year 503, and founded a distinct kingdom, which

lished therein, differs little from the Lowland Scotish, and neither of them so much from common English, as the Lancashire or Exmoor dialect will be found to do; whereas, had the Pictish been Gothic, and the Buchan the Pictish, the difference between that dialect and the English would at this moment have been as wide and radical at least as that which exists between the languages of England and Denmark or Sweden.[*] Mr Pinkerton, in his very interesting "Enquiry into the History of Scotland," 1789, has been pleased not only to contend that the Picts were Goths, but to be very lavish in his abuse upon those who have dared to think otherwise. A complete refutation of this hypothesis would require a large volume, and must be expected from some able hand; but no one, in the meantime, can refrain from lamenting that a discussion so curious and important, and in the course of which the inquirer has evinced uncommon industry and singular acuteness, should be degraded by groundless assertion, absurd prejudice, scurrilous language, and diabolical malignity.[†] Mr Pinkerton's only argument, setting aside his fulminations of *fool, blockhead,* &c., which do not, with submission, appear entitled to that appellation, is, that because the Picts came from Scandinavia they were consequently Scythians, which by no means follows, since the "Celtic savages" (as he is pleased to call them) had peopled all that country long before his favourite Goths arrived in it.

---

[*] "For the wonderful affinity between the Swedish and English, see Mr Coxe's 'Travels.' Had Sweden been where Ireland is, the Swedish would also have been called English." ! ! ! ("Essay on the Origin of Scotish Poetry," prefixed to "Ancient Scotish Songs," p. lxx. 1786.

[†] See his treatment of the Celts, wild Irish, and Highlanders, *passim.* To suppose a particular people, who, in genius and virtue, are inferior to none upon earth, intended by nature "as a medial race between beasts and men," and seriously propose methods "to get rid of the breed," argues a being of "a medial race" between devil and man. The author has been thought to be possessed with an incubus; he would seem also to have been engendered by one.

lasted till the year 843, when, either by victory or descent, by force or fraud, their king, Kenneth III., surnamed, from his father, MacAlpin, acquired the dominion of the Picts; who, however, continued, at least in Galloway, a distinct people till about the middle of the eleventh century, after which they are no longer mentioned by any historian, or in any public document, or other writing; their name and language so entirely disappearing, as if, according to Innes, the whole race had been cut off like a man that leaves no posterity: which gave occasion to an ancient author to say that, even in his time, what was recorded of them seemed a mere fable;* and has led others to imagine that every soul of them had been extirpated by the triumphant Scots. The country, then called Albany, in about a century and a half from this event, obtained the name of Scotland, by which it has been ever since known; but it is to be considered that (except in the northernmost parts, where the Danes or Norwegians had gained some footing, and, perhaps, in the Merse and Lothians, which were for some time in the possession of the English Saxons) the speech and manners of the inhabitants were universally Celtic, or, in a word, nearly those of the Highlanders, as they are called, at this day. From the period of this union, the Pictish language seems to have yielded to the courtly ascendancy of the Gaelic, being no longer noticed, at least, as a distinct idiom, and the transition, in fact, from one tongue to the other

---

* H. Huntingdon. "Scrip. post Bedam," p. 299. 1596. Innes, i. 147. See also the preceding note.

being the more easy and natural from the assimilation or affinity of the two dialects.°

Malcolm III., surnamed *Cean-more*, or great-head, ascended the throne of Scotland in 1056. This monarch, during the usurpation of his predecessor Macbeth, resided for many years at the court of Edward, called the Confessor, king of England, by whom he was assisted in his attempt to recover the crown. He married an English princess; and preferring, it is probable, the more polished manners and refined language of the Anglo-Saxons to those of his own countrymen, gave such encouragement to their introduction, that it is to this period and these events we are to attribute the rapid decline and gradual abolition of the Gaelic or old Scotish as the national language; for cultivated it does not appear and is not supposed to have been at any period whatever.† What Malcolm thus began, his suc-

* Innes, "Essay," i. 147. The Irish language would have the greater superiority over the Pictish from its being written, which we have no reason to think was the case with the latter.

† Many other circumstances concurred in producing this great change. The Saxon nobility found a hospitable reception at the court of Malcolm in 1066, ("Annals of Scotland," by Lord Hailes, i. 11;) while the piety of his consort, who had great influence over him, would be a sufficient inducement for the monks and priests, a species of vermin with which England at that time swarmed, to solicit her patronage and protection. Numbers, likewise, of the Northumbrian Saxons sought an asylum in Scotland on their country being ravaged by the Norman tyrant in 1080, (S. Dunelm. 199. "Annals," i. 11.) Besides, Malcolm himself, in an irruption he made into England in 1070, brought home such a number of captives that his land was almost filled with English servants, not a village or hovel, according to the monk of Durham, being for many years to be found without them, ("Annals," i. 10.) William of

B

cessors completed ; all till Alexander II. receiving an English education, learning the English language, and marrying English princesses.

Newborough, too, who wrote about the year 1200, mentions that there was in the army of William King of Scots (1173) a great number of English, for, says he, the towns and boroughs of the Scotish kingdom are known to be inhabited by the English. The Scots, he adds, taking the occasion of the king's absence, revealed their innate hatred against them, which they had dissembled for fear of the king, and slew as many as they could find, those who could escape flying to the royal castles, (Pinkerton's "Enquiry," i. 345.) This author seems to have magnified some accidental quarrel between the Scots and English settlers into a general massacre. "Our eldaris," says the translator of Boethius, "(quhilkis dwelt continewally merchand with the realme of Ingland) lernit the Saxonis toung be frequent ieoperdeis and chance of battall sustenit mony zeris aganis thaym." A little lower he adds—"Bechance of sindry seasonis specially about the tyme of King Malcolme Canmore, al thingis began to change. For quhen oure nychtbouris the Brytonis war maid effeminat be lang sleuth, and doung out of Britane be the Saxonis in Walis, we began to haue alliance be proximite of Romanis with Inglysmen, specially efter the exterminioun of Pichtis, and be frequent and dayly cumpany of thaym we began to rute thair langage, and superflew maneris in oure brestis," ("History of Scotland," sig. D, ii. b. Edin., 1541.) To these facts must be added the actual superiority of the Saxon language. The Scots at this period were so excessively illiterate, that even their sovereign himself, as we learn from one who knew him, was unable to read, ("Annals," i. 13.) The Saxons, on the contrary, were a very literary people, and cultivated their native tongue with equal assiduity and success. The churchmen and other refugees would of course carry a number of books into Scotland, and, being familiar with the modes of education, could teach the natives Saxon with much greater facility and expedition than they could possibly acquire the Gaelic. Had the former been as little of a written or cultivated language as the latter, it would never have withstood the shock of the invasion, authority, arts, and influence of the Norman conquerors, and French would at this moment have been the mother tongue of

That the Gaelic language was spoken, or at least well understood, at the court of Malcolm III., is a fact not to be disputed; since, to lay no stress on his own nick-name, and the epithet of *bane*, or fair, bestowed on his brother Donald, we are most fortunately in possession of a *duan*, or poem, in that tongue, which is supposed to have been written by the royal bard, or poet-laureate of the time, and most probably soon after his accession. In this invaluable curiosity the poet addresses his countrymen by the title of Albans, and enumerates the ancestors of the reigning monarch up to Albanus, the first (imaginary) possessor. " Ye knowing men of Alba," says he, " ye comely hosts of the yellow tresses,* know ye the first ' possessors ' of that country? Albanus of the numerous combatants was the first possessor. He was the son of Isiacon ; from him is derived the name of Alba," &c. " Malcolm, son of Donchad," he concludes, " is the present king. God alone knows how long he is to reign. To the present time, of the son of

---

an Englishman : which, to speak without prejudice, would, so far from being a subject for lamentation, have made some amends for the chicane, barbarism, and tyranny they have introduced into a free and simple constitution. See more on the subject of the introduction of the English language into Scotland in Sir John Sinclair's " Observations on the Scottish Dialect," p. 8, 1782, and the "Transactions of the Society of the Antiquaries of Scotland," pp. 168, 408. And thus, as Mr Pinkerton observes, " has the vulgar error crept in, that the Scotish is derived from the Anglo-Saxon, or that it is in fact merely a dialect of the English imported into that country."

* How is this reconcileable with Mr Pinkerton's assertion, that " flaxen, *yellow*, and red hair," are the distinguishing features of the Goths, as " *black* curled hair and brown faces are of the Celts ?" (" Enquiry," i. 26, 340.)

Donchad the lively-faced, fifty-two kings of the race of Erk have reigned over Alba."*

It is not, indeed, probable that the English language became all at once, or even during the reign of Malcolm, who died in 1093, the common speech of the people; but the innovations then made were productive of such consequences, that in the time of Alexander III., A.D. 1249, the language of the two countries differed, if at all, only in dialect; the Gaelic in one, like the Welsh and Cornish in the other, being confined to the remote and mountainous parts, of which the inhabitants were less civilised or commercial.† That the old Scotish was still understood, though it had ceased to be spoken at court, appears from a curious circumstance. At the coronation of this monarch, an ancient Highlander saluted him in that language, with his pedigree or genealogy carried back to a remote period. ‡

* See it at full length, the original and two translations, in Pinkerton's "Enquiry," ii. p. 321, and an account of it, p. 106. "It appears," says this writer, in a different publication, from Turgot's "Life of St Margaret," "that the king was interpreter between her and the Scotish ecclesiastics. If they spoke Gaelic," he adds, "the king would not have understood them, for he had been seventeen years in England, where he had only spoken French, and Saxon to servants." Mr P. perhaps resided in the English court at that period. He, however, with uncommon candour, allows that "this argument is not strong," which will doubtless prevent every other person from pronouncing it ridiculous and absurd.

† These, however, are presumed to have been, in Scotland, if not a considerable majority of the people, at least possessors of the greatest part of the kingdom, for many centuries after this event. See Stillingfleet's "Origines Britannicæ," p. 252. 1685.

‡ See Fordun's "Scotichronicon," p. 759, (Hearne's edition;) Major's "Historia Britanniæ," p. 151, (1740;) "In Lingua Hiber-

An investigation of the poetry and song of the ancient inhabitants of this country, whether Picts or Scots,

nica," says the latter, "et non nostra Scotorum Meridionalium Anglicana." The expression of Fordun's continuator is merely "hiis Scoticis verbis." The vulgar language of the Lowland Scots was always called English by their own writers till a late period. Thus, in the "Flyting of Dunbar and Kennedie," (about 1500,) in the "Ever-Green," vol. ii. p. 53, the former says—

> " I haif on me a pair of Lowthiane hipps
> Sall fairer Inglis mak, and mair perfet
> Thau thou can blebber with thy Carrick lipps."

the Erse, or Irish, being the dialect of that province. So also the same Dunbar, in his "Golden Terge"—

> " O reverend Chawser, rose of rethouris all,
> Was thou not of our Inglis all the licht?"

Again, in Sir David Lyndsay's " Prologue to the Complaint of the Papingo "—

> " Alace for ane, quhilk lamp was in this land,
> Of eloquence the flowand balmy strand,
> And in our Inglis rhetorick the rose,
> As of rubeis the carbunckle bin chose,
> And as Phebus dois Cynthia precell,
> So Gawin Douglas bishop of Dunkell," &c.

Yet Douglas is certainly the most Scotified of all the Scotish poets extant.

Again, in the same author's " Satyre of the Thrie Estaits : "

> " *Qui non laborat non manducet.*
> This is in Inglische toung or leit:
> Quha labouris nocht he sall not eit."

Again, in the "Act for allowing the Bible in the Vulgar Tongue," p. 154—"It is statute and ordanit, that it sall be lefull to our savirane Ladyis lieges to haif the haly writ, to wit, the New Testament and the Auld, in the vulgar toung in Inglis or Scottis, of ane gude and true translatioun," &c. Here *Scottis*, as in the quotation from Fordun, must necessarily mean *Irish*. Mr John Pinkerton, however, has been pleased to assert that "the Scotish . . . . is mentioned by all its early writers as a different language from the Southern or English," an assertion which, like most others of that ingenious gentleman, wants nothing but truth to support it.

previous to the introduction and establishment of the English language, would no doubt be curious and interesting; but, unfortunately, no remains or vestiges thereof are now to be met with. Many pieces of Erse * or Gaelic poetry have, it is true, been lately collected and published, which are said to have great merit, but cannot well be of the antiquity they pretend to; every one at least is, or ought to be, now satisfied that the epic poems of Òssian, who is supposed to have existed in the fifth century, as professedly translated by Mr Macpherson, are chiefly, if not wholly, of his own invention.† The song, therefore, which is meant to be

---

* The word *Erse* is used to mean the Irish language, as written or spoken in the Highlands and Isles of Scotland, (Irish, *Erish, Ersh, Erse.*) The natives of those parts distinguish their dialect by the name of Gaelic-Albanich from that of the Irish, which they call Gaelic-Erinach. The Lowland Scots having been taught, as above related, to speak English, began to look upon their countrymen who still adhered to the ancient language as Irish, a name given them by Barbour in his "Life of Bruce," written 1375, and continued till at least the middle of the sixteenth century. See the "Flyting of Dunbar and Kennedie," in the "Ever-Green," vol. ii. pp. 53, 66; and the "Letters and Negociations of Sir Ralph Sadler," pp. 263, 334. Edinburgh, 1720.

† The late Dr Samuel Johnson always strenuously denied their authenticity, of which, however, had his resolution or corporal strength been different from what it was, the author or editor would have effectually convinced him by a well-known argument—the *ultima ratio* of a convicted impostor. The only translations of Erse poetry, unattended with circumstances of fraud or suspicion, appeared some years ago in the *Gentleman's Magazine*, and were afterward privately reprinted by the ingenious and industrious collector. Several volumes of songs and poems in that language have, it is true, been published between these forty or fifty years, * but not

---

* "Ais-eiridh na sean chánoin Albannaich," &c., le Alastair Mac-Dhonuill.

the subject of this essay is that of the natives of Scotland speaking and writing the English language.

being accompanied with an English version, (which, however,
would, if close and faithful, be infinitely more curious, and even
valuable, than the pretended works of Ossian in the Klopstockian
bombast of Mr Macpherson,) must remain confined to the Highland gentry, for whom they are intended, as no others, it is believed,
have been yet induced to study the originals. See also an interesting paper by Dr Young, upon the subject of Ossian, in the "Transactions of the Royal Irish Academy," vol. i. Many pamphlets,
and indeed books, were published in the course of the controversy
respecting the genuineness of Ossian, by Dr Blair, Duff, Smith,
Shaw, Clarke, Macnicol, and others; but scarcely any of them
seems worthy of being consulted or referred to for the sake of information. Dr Blair is well known as an elegant and masterly writer;
but it is believed he would find it much easier to write a hundred
critical dissertations upon the authenticity of these poems, than to
prove it in half a dozen pages by argument and evidence, as the
literati of every other country would, in a similar case, have thought
it necessary to do. It seems both unreasonable and arrogant that
the Scotish writers alone should expect all the world to be satisfied
with their naked assertions upon a subject in which interest or par-
tiality must naturally render their testimony suspected; but, indeed,
as not one single Erse manuscript, either ancient or modern, (and
Mr Macpherson pretended to have several,) has been yet deposited
in any public library, or even seen by any person of veracity, the
question seems completely decided, though not much to the honour
of that gentleman, his advocates, or adherents. An inquiry, however, into the history of Gaelic song by a person of integrity and
abilities, possessed of a competent knowledge of the language, who
should prefer fact to opinion, authority to conjecture, and fidelity to
fine writing, would be unquestionably curious and interesting, and
is anxiously desired, the Celtic nations having been ever celebrated
for their poetical genius, a character which their present Irish and

---

12mo, Duneidiunn, 1751. "Orain Ghaidhealach," le Donchadh Mac-an-t-saior,
12mo, Dun-eidin, 1768. "Comh-chruinnea-adh orinnaigh Gaidhealach," le
Roanuill Macdomhnuill, 8vo, Duneidiunn, 1776. "Sean dain, agus orain
Ghaidhealach," 8vo, Peart, 1786. These, beside the "Sean dana," published,
under very suspicious circumstances, by Dr Smith, in 1787, are all, it is believed,
that have hitherto appeared.

The earliest specimen of Scotish song now remaining
is fortunately preserved in the rhyming chronicle of Andrew Winton, prior of Lochleven, written, as is generally
supposed, about the year 1420; where, speaking of the
great plenty of corn and victual in the time of king
Alexander III., who was killed by a fall from his horse
in 1285–6, he says,

> " This falyhyd fra he deyd suddanly,
>   This sang wes made off hym for thi.
>   Quhen Alysander oure kynge wes dede,
>   That Scotland led in luwe and le,
>   Away wes sons off ale and brede,
>   Off wyne and wax, off gamyn and gle :
>   Oure gold wes changyd into lede :
>   Cryst, borne into vergyynyte,
>   Succour Scotland, and remede
>   That stad in his perplexite !"*

Highland descendants, however enslaved, oppressed, vilified, and
degraded, have by no means forfeited. " It is no uncommon thing,"
says the author of some MS. letters on the Celtic language, and
" An Enquiry into the Original, &c., of the Ancient Scots," written
in 1756, (he means in Ireland, or the Highlands,) "to hear a shepherd following his flocks, or a maid with a 'pail' of milk on her
head, diverting themselves with songs of their own composition,
worthy of being known to the world both for the purity of the dic-
tion, the sublimity of their images, and all the most essential graces
of composition." The writer, whose name is Stone, was school-
master of Dunkeld, and published some translations from the Gaelic,
which (like many other translators from that language) he appears
from this MS. not to have understood. Mr Buchanan, in his lately
published "Travels in the Western Hebrides," p. 80, is still more
elaborate and decided in their praise. Even the simple sequestered
natives of St Kilda, according to Martin, " have a genius for poesie,
and compose entertaining verses and songs in their own language,
[the Irish,] which is very emphatical." See also Macaulay's "History," p. 216; Buchanan's "Travels," p. 139.

* MSS. Reg. 17, DXX. No direct evidence, it is presumed, can
be adduced of the vulgar language of the south of Scotland anterior
to the above date.

The next is one of four lines upon the siege of Berwick by the English monarch in the year 1296. "King Edward," says an ancient chronicler, "went him toward Berwyke, and biseged the toune, and tho that were with yn manlich hem defended, and sett on fire and brent two of the king Edwarde shippes, and seide in dispite and reprefe of him :

> 'Wend kyng Edewarde, with his lange shankes,
> To have gete Berwyke, al our unthankes?
> Gas pikes hym,
> And after gas dikes hym.'"

This pleasantry, however, as hath been elsewhere observed, was in the present instance somewhat ill-timed ; for as soon as the king heard of it, he assaulted the town with such fury, that he carried it with the loss of 25,700 Scots.*

That many songs of this age have formerly existed there can be no doubt. The heroic Wallace was the subject of several ; some of which are expressly referred

---

* MSS. Har., 226, 7333. See also P. Langtoft, p. 272; " Ancient Songs," p. xxxi., 1790. The number seems prodigiously exaggerated. Winton makes it only 7500 ; though Boece (or his translator) observes, "that ane mil mycht haif gane two days ithandlie be stremis of blude." In order to show the affinity, or rather identity, of the two languages at this period, it may not be impertinent to transcribe the sarcasm which some Englishman made a few weeks after "in reprefe of the Scottes," on their losing the battie of Dunbar—

> " Thus scaterand Scottis
> Hold 1 for sootis,
> Of wrenchis unware ;
> Eerly in a mornyng,
> In an euyl tyding,
> Went ze froo Dunnbarre."

to, as evidence of an historical fact, in certain copies of Fordun's "Scotichronicon." *

The battle of Bannockburn, which proved so fatal to English ambition, in 1314, is well known. "On this occasion," says Fabyan, "the Scottes enflamed with pride, in derysyon of the Englyshmen, made this ryme as foloweth :

> 'Maydens of Englande, sore may ye morne,
>　For your lemmans ye have lost at Bannockysborne,
>　　With heue a lowe.
>　What ! weneth the king of England
>　So soone to have wone Scotlande ?
>　　Wyth rumbylowe.'"

"Thys songe," he adds, "was after many daies song in daunces in the carols of the maidens and mynstrelles of Scotland, to the reprofe and disdayne of Englyshemen, with dyuers others, whych," says he, "I ouerpasse." †

---

* See Goodall's edition, vol. ii. p. 176.　The editor has heard it gravely asserted in Edinburgh, that a foolish song, beginning—

> " Go, go, go, go to Berwick, Johny,
>　Thou shall have the horse, and I 'll have the poney,"

was actually made upon one of this hero's marauding expeditions, and that the person thus addressed was no other than his *fidus Achates*, Sir John Graham.

† These lines, certainly not inelegant for the time, nor improper for the occasion, occur, with some trifling variance, in MS. Har., 226, and in Caxton's " Chronicle," c. 58.　His words are—" Wherfor the Scottes said in reproue and despite of Kyng Edward, for as moche as he loued to gone by water, and also for he was disconfited at Bannokesborne, therfor maydens maden a song therof in that contre of Kyng Edward of Englond, and in this maner they songe—'Maydens of England, sare may ye morne, for tizt haue ye lost your lammans at Bannockesborne, with heualogh.　What wende the Kyng of England to haue get Scotland with rombilong.'"　The MS. reads—

> " For tynt ze lost your lemmanes at Bannockesborne, with heilfelows : "

In 13—, Sir John de Soulis, the Scotish governor of Eskdale, with fifty men, defeated a body of three hundred, commanded by Sir Andrew Hercla, who was taken prisoner: and the rhyming historian Barbour forbears to "reherss the maner" of the victory, as, he says,

> " Quhasa liks thai may her
> Young women, quhen thai will play,
> Syng it amang thaim ilk day." *

In the year 1328, being the second of our Edward III., David, son of Robert de Brus, king of Scots, married Jane of the Tower, or Joan of Towers, sister to King Edward; which marriage, confirming the peace lately made between the two nations, and which the English considered as inadequate and dishonourable, "it was not long," says Fabyan, " or the Scottes, in dispite of the English menne, called her Jane Make-peace; and also to their more derision, thei made diuerse truffes, roundes, and songes, of the whiche," he adds, "one is specially remembred as foloweth :

> ' Long beerdis hartles,
> Paynted hoodes wytles,
> Gay cottes gracelcs,
> Maketh Englande thryfteless.'

Which ryme, as saieth Guydo, was made by the Scottes, princypally for the deformyte of clothyng that at those dayes was vsed by Englysshemenne." †

so that *tynt* was probably the original word, and *lost* originally a gloss. *Hcve and how rombelow* appears to have been formerly the ordinary burthen of a ballad, as *Derrydown* is at present. See Skelton's Works, p. 67, 1736; Percy's "Reliques," vol. ii. p. 49; "Ancient Songs," p. li., 1790; Johnson's "Scots Musical Museum."

   * "The Bruce," vol. iii. p. 49.

   † Master Caxton gives a somewhat different account of the mat-

Hume of Godscroft relates that "the lord of Liddesdale, being at his pastime, hunting in Attrick forest, is
beset by William, Earl of Douglas, and such as hee had
ordained for that purpose, and there assailed, wounded,
and slain beside Galsewood, in the yeare 1353, upon a
jealousie that the earle had conceived of him with his
lady, as the report goeth ; for so sayes the old song:

> ' The countesse of Douglas out of her boure she came,
> And loudly there that she did call ;
> It is for the lord of Liddesdale
> That I let all these teares downefall.' "

"The song," continues he, "also declareth how shee
did write her love letters to Liddisdale to disswade him
from that hunting. It tells likewise the manner of the
taking of his men, and his owne killing at Galsewood,
and how hee was carried the first night to Lindin kirk,
a mile from Selkirk, and was buried within the abbacie
of Melrosse."* This song, if extant, must be a prodigious curiosity.

ter; for, says he, "at Estren next after his coronacion the kyng
ordeyned an huge hoste for to fight agens the Scottes, ... and
the Scottes came 'to York' to the kyng, for to make pees and
accord; but the accordement betwene hem last but a litell tyme,
and at that time the Englishmen were clothed all in cotes and hodes
peynted with lettres and with flours full semely, with long berdes,
and therefor the Scottes made a bile that was fastened upon the
chirch-dores of Seint Petre toward Stangate, and thus said the
scripture in despite of Englishmen—

> ' Long herde hertheles, peynted hood wytlees,
> Gay cote graceles, makes Englond thriftlees.' "

These lines, it must be confessed, have not much the appearance of
a *rounde* or *songe;* and as to the nature of a *truffe*, we are left altogether in the dark. See also Fuller's "Worthies," p. 86.

* "History of the Houses of Douglas and Angus," p. 77, Edin.,

King James I., who was born in 1393, and became
entitled to the crown on the death of his father, Robert
III., in 1405, but having been taken at sea a few months
before, on his passage for France, and most unjustly
detained a prisoner in England for nineteen years, was
not restored till 1424, is celebrated by Major as an
excellent composer of Scotish songs, a number of his
performances being still popular in the time of that historian.   He particularly mentions an artificial song beginning " Yas sen," &c., and also that pleasant and
artificial song " At Beltayn," which some persons, he
says, at Dalkeith and Gargeil, had attempted to parody,
by reason of his having been shut up in a tower or
chamber in which a woman resided with her mother.*
The latter of these poems, for it does not seem to
answer the definition of a song, is fortunately preserved,
and hath been lately given to the public. †   This accomplished prince was murdered in 1437.

1644.   Liddesdale was a Douglas, and natural son to the good Sir
James, who, in his way to Jerusalem with Bruce's heart, A.D. 1330,
was killed in Spain by the Moors.   He was commonly called " The
Flower of Chivalry."   Lord Hailes (" Annals," vol. ii. p. 161,
et seq.) calls him only the " Knight of Liddesdale ; " has " Galvorde"
instead of " Galsewood ; " mentions the assassination as being done
in revenge for the murder of Alexander Ramsay and David Berke-
ley ; and says that Liddesdale left a widow, who afterwards married
Hugh, brother of William, Lord Dacre.

* " De Gestis Scotorum," l. vi.

† See " Select Scotish Ballads," vol. ii., and " The Caledonian
Muse," (when published.)   There is likewise reason to suspect that
the words *Yas sen* are corruptly given for *Sen yat;* in which case
this piece will also be found in print.   See " Ancient Scotish
Poems," vol. ii. p. 214, 1786.   It begins :

" Sen that [the] eyne, that workis my weilfaire ; "

In that truly excellent composition, "At Beltayn; or, Peblis to the Play," the royal author has referred to some popular songs of his own time, which may be thought to deserve notice, though now irretrievably lost. Thus, in stanza the sixth:

> " Ane zoung man stert into that steid,
> Als cant as ony colt,
> Ane birkin hat vpon his heid,
> With ane bow and ane bolt ;
> Said, mirrie madinis, think nocht lang,
> The wedder is fair and smolt
> He cleikit vp ane hie ruf sang,
> Thair fure ane man to the holt,
>   Quod he.
> Of Peblis to the play."

Again, in stanza the twenty-fifth:

> " He fippillit lyk ane faderles fole,
> And [said] be still, my sweit thing.—
> Be the haly rud of Peblis,
> I may nocht rest for greting.—
> He quhissilit and he pypit bayth,
> To mak hir blyth that meiting :
> My hony hart, how sayis the sang ?
> Thair sal be mirth at our meting
>   Zit.
> Of Peblis to the play."

In some of the prologues to the admirable translation of Virgil by Gawin Douglas, Bishop of Dunkeld, in 1513, several songs are mentioned, which were doubtless popular, and probably ancient at that time. Thus, for instance, in the prologue to Book XII.:

> " On salt stremes wolk Dorida and Thetis
> By rynnand strandis, nymphes and Naiades,
> Sic as we clepe wenschis and damyssellis,
> In gersy grauis wanderand by spring wellis,
> Of blomed branschis and flouris quhyte and rede
> Plettand thare lusty chaplettis for thare hede :

and, though consisting of thirteen long stanzas, is much more of a song than the other.

Sum sang ring sangis, dancis, ledis and roundis,
With vocis schil, quhil all the dale resoundis ;
Quhareso thay walk into thare karoling,
For amourus layis dois all the rochis ring
Ane sang, 'The schip salis ouer the salt fame,
Will bring thir merchandis and my lemane hame.'
Sun vther singis, 'I will be blyith and licht,
My hert is lent apoun sa gudly wicht.'"

Again, in the same prologue :

" Our awin natiue bird, gentil dow,
Singand on hir kynde, 'I come hidder to wow.'"

Again, in the prologue to Book XIII. :

" Thareto thir birdis singis in thare schawis,
As menstralis playis, 'The ioly day now dawis.'" *

The "Flowers of the Forest," a song commemorative

* This song or tune appears to have been very famous. The poet
Dunbar, in a satirical address to the merchants of Edinburgh, (MSS.
More, Ll. 5, 10,) says,

" Your commone menstralls hes no tone,
Bot 'Now the day dawis,' and 'Into Joun.'"

In "The Muses Threnodie," p. 146, Perth, 1774, these words,
" Hey the day now dawnes," are quoted as the name of "a cele-
brated old Scotch song," as indeed it must be, if the same with that
mentioned by Bishop Douglas. In "The Life and Death of the
Piper of Kilbarchan ; or, The Epitaph of Habbie Simson," ("Scots
Poems," 1706,) is the following line :

" Now, who shall play 'The day it daws?'"

The tune may therefore, it is highly probable, be still known to
pipers ; and if so, might be yet recovered. There is some doubt,
however, after all, whether the song or tune be actually, or at least
originally, Scotish. In the Fairrax MS., a collection of musical
pieces made about the year 1500, is a song of two stanzas, written,
it should seem, out of compliment to Queen Elizabeth, daughter of
Edward IV., and wife to Henry VII., the first of which is as follows :

" This day day dawes,
This gentil day dawes,
And I must home gone.

" In a glorious garden grene,
Saw I sytting a comly quene,

of the battle of Flodden, in 1513, and inserted in the
present collection, must, if actually of that age, be
allowed a much finer specimen of lyric elegy than the
English language is able to produce at so early a period.*
Its antiquity, however, has been called in question; and

> Among the flouris that fresh byn:
> She gadered a floure and sett betwene,
>   The lyly whyzt rose methought I sawe,
>   And ever she sang,
>   This day day dawes,
>   This gentil day dawes."

See it in a collection of "Ancient Songs in Score," fol., 1779.
The music is nothing more than mere drawling chants in counter-
point, without the slightest pretension to melody; so that it would
seem as if either the English harmonist had entirely spoiled the
Scotish tune, or the Scotish piper had considerably improved the
English one.

  * Mr Tytler, in his ingenious but fanciful "Dissertation on the
Scotish Music,"* speaks of "The Souters of Selkirk" as an old
song, composed on the same occasion. "This ballad," he adds,
in a note, "is founded on the following incident:—Previous to the
battle of Flowden, the town-clerk of Selkirk conducted a band of
eighty souters, or shoemakers, of that town, who joined the royal
army; and the town-clerk, in reward of his loyalty, was created a
knight-banneret by that prince. They fought gallantly, and were
most of them cut off. A few who escaped, found on their return in
the forest of Ladywood-edge the wife of one of their brethren lying
dead, and her child sucking her breast. Thence the town of Selkirk obtained for their arms, a woman sitting upon a sarcophagus
holding a child in her arms; in the background a wood; and on
the sarcophagus the arms of Scotland." For all this fine story there
is probably no foundation whatever. That the souters of Selkirk
should, in 1513, amount to fourscore fighting men, is a circumstance
utterly incredible. It is scarcely to be supposed that all the shoemakers in Scotland could have produced such an army, at a period

  * Printed (1) at the end of Arnot's "History of Edinburgh," 1779; (2) with
the "Poetical Remains of James I.," 1783; (3) by way of preface to Napier's
"Collection of Scots Songs;" and, lastly, in the "Transactions of the Society
of the Antiquaries of Scotland," 1792

the fact is, that no copy, printed or manuscript, so old as the beginning of the present century, can be now produced.

King James V. is well known as the reputed author of two songs of great merit—the "Gaberlunzieman," and the "Beggar's Meal Pokes," both inserted in the present collection, and said to have been composed on two of his own adventures : this prince (whose character, Dr Percy thinks, for wit and libertinism bears a great resemblance to that of his gay successor, Charles II.) being noted for strolling about his dominions in dis-

---

when shoes must have been still less worn than they are at present. Dr Johnson, indeed, was told at Aberdeen that the people learned the art of making shoes from Cromwell's soldiers. "The numbers," he adds, "that go barefoot are still sufficient to show that shoes may be spared : they are not yet considered as necessaries of life : for tall boys, not otherwise meanly dressed, run without them in the streets; and in the islands the sons of gentlemen pass several of their first years with naked feet," ("Journey to the Western Islands," p. 55.) Away, then, with the fable of "The Souters of Selkirk!" Mr Tytler, though he mentions it as the subject of a song or ballad, does not "remember ever to have seen the original genuine words," as he obligingly acknowledged in a letter to the editor. Mr Robertson, however, who gives the statistical account of the parish of Selkirk, seems to know something more of the matter. "Some," says he, "have very falsely attributed to this event [the battle of Flowden] that song,

"Up with the souters of Selkirk, and down with the Earl of Hume."
"There was no Earl of Hume," he adds, "at that time, nor was this song composed till long after. It arose from a bet betwixt the Philiphaugh and Hume families; the souters (or shoemakers) of Selkirk against the men of Hume, at a match of football, in which the souters of Selkirk completely gained, and afterwards perpetuated their victory in that song." This is decisive; and so much for Scotish tradition.

C

guise,* and for his frequent gallantries with country girls. It is of the latter of these ballads that Mr Walpole has remarked, there is something very ludicrous in the young woman's distress when she thought her first favours had been thrown away upon a beggar.

His most, and most justly, celebrated performance, however, is, "Christ's Kirk on the Green," in which he rivalled, or indeed eclipsed, the fame of his great ancestor's once equally popular production, "At Beltayn," &c. This, indeed, like the latter, is rather a poem than a song, and has been accordingly printed as such in a collection which ought to have made its appearance many years ago.†

---

* "Sc. of a tinker, beggar, &c. Thus he used to visit a smith's daughter at Niddry, near Edinburgh," ("Reliques," ii., 60.) Scottish writers have repeatedly cited the compliments paid, or supposed to be paid, to this monarch, by Ariosto and Ronsard; but no one has ever cited, or perhaps observed, the following passage in the "Scaligerana," which may serve to identify or correct his portrait: "*Le roy d'Ecosse, Jacques V. estoit camard, ce qui estoit bien laid, quia nasus honestamentum faciei.*"

† "Caledonian Muse," printed for J. Johnson, St Paul's Churchyard, in 1785. This poem has been erroneously ascribed to James I. See an essay on the true author, in the publication referred to. A voluminous writer, who deals largely in premeditated falsehood, absurd opinions, and confident assertions, positively affirms that "there were three poems of this kind, all by James I.—this; 'Falkland on the Grene;' 'Peblis to the Play.' The first and last," he says, "are preserved; and one refers to the rural manners of the north of Scotland; and is composed in the Scandinavian alliteration, and with many Norse words. The other, or 'Peblis,' to those of the south of Scotland; and is full of the southern Scotish, or north English, words of old metrical romances. 'Falkland,'" he adds, "is unfortunately lost; but we may well suppose it described the sports of Fifeshire, or the middle of Scotland, in words adapted to that part." It only remains for this ingenious romancer to add to

The ballad of "Johnny Armstrong," inserted in this collection, is probably coeval with the death of that gallant freebooter.*

The affair of Solway Moss, in 1542, is generally thought to have hastened the king's death. The Scotish lords taken prisoners on this occasion were liberated by King Henry upon pledges, and appear, from a passage in Sir Ralph Sadler's Letters, to have become very unpopular. "The Earl of Glencairn," says he, "prayed me to write to your majesty, and to beseech the same for the passion of God, to encourage them so much as to give them trust, for they were already commonly hated here for your majesty's sake, and throughout the realm called the English lords; and such ballads and songs made of them, how the English angels had corrupted them, as have not been heard."† None of these, it is believed, are now to be met with.

"Where Helen Lyes," a song, as it is supposed, of this age, will be found in the present collection.

In the year 1549, a singular performance was published at St Andrews, which affords considerable information as to the state of Scotish song at that period. It

his numerous forgeries the imaginary poem of "Falkland on the Grene."

   * The Rev. Mr Boyd, the ingenious translator of Dante, has a faint recollection of a ballad "on some Armstrong, (not the well-known ballad of 'Johny Armstrong,' in Ramsay's 'Evergreen;')" another called "Johny Cox;" and another "of a Scotch minstrel, who stole a horse from some of the Henries of England." The first of these ballads is possibly the famous old Border song of "Dick o' the Cow," quoted by Mr Pennant, ("Tour," 1772, part 2, p. 276,) and printed at length in "The Poetical Museum," Hawick, 1784.

   † P. 198.

is entitled, " Vedderburn's * Complainte of Scotlande,
vyth ane exortatione to the thre estaits to be vigilant in
the deffens of their public veil ;" and is dedicated to the
queen dowager regent.   Whoever this Wedderburn was,
his work has been usually, though doubtless untruly,
ascribed to Sir James Inglis, a celebrated writer about
that time.   The book is so very rare and curious, not
above a single copy of it being known to exist, that
the reader, it is hoped, will not be dissatisfied with the
length of the following extract.   The author, become
weak and sad through study, supposes himself, for the
sake of recreation, to pass "to the green holsum fields,"
where he observes the birds and beasts, and describes
the sounds they uttered ; he is also witness to an engagement between two ships, of which he likewise gives
a minute description.   He then proceeds as follows :—
" The reik, smuik, and the stink of the gunpuldir fylit all
the ayr . . . quhilk generit sik mirknes and myst that
i culd nocht see my lyntht about me, quharfor i rais
and returnit to the fresche feildis . . . quhar i beheld
mony hudit hirdis blauuand ther buc hornis and ther

---

* *Vedderburn*, for *Wedderburn ;* the *v* being almost everywhere
substituted for the *w;* not, as a certain eccentric writer absurdly
conjectures, because the types were brought from France, (as if a
w could not have been made of *vv*, as it actually is, in some instances, of *uu ;*) but because it was the dialect of that and the preceding centuries, not in Scotland only, but in the north of England ;
though now a peculiarity of the London cockneys.   (See " Sir Ralph
Sadler's Letters," &c., p. 20; also a curious warrant of King James
I. in Morgan's " Phœnix Britannicus," p. 54, and some old songs
used in the Bishoprick of Durham, MSS., Harl., 7578.)   It is,
however, less accountable that the *w* is not, with equal impropriety,
printed for the *v*.

corne pipis, calland and conuoyand mony fat floc to be
fed on the feldis ; than the scheiphirdis pat there scheip
on bankis and brais, and on dry hillis, to get ther pastour. Than i beheld the scheiphirdis vyuis and ther
childir that brocht there mornyng bracfast to the scheiphirdis. . . . Than after there disiune tha began to talk
of grit myrrynes that was rycht plesand to be hard. In
the fyrst the prencipal scheiphirde made ane orisone tyl
al the laif of his compangzons as eftir follouis." The
subject is a description of the universe. "Quhen the
scheipherd hed endit his prolixt orison to the laif of the
scheiphirdis, i meruellit nocht litil, quhen i herd ane
rustic pastour of bestialite, distitut of vrbanite and of
speculatione of natural philosophe, indoctryne his nycht-
bours as he hed studeit Ptholome, Auerois, Aristotel,
Galien, Ypocrites, or Cicero, quhilk var expert practicians
in methamatic art. Than the scheiphirdis vyf said, my
veil belouit hisband, i pray the to decist fra that tideus
melancolic orison quhilk surpassis thy ingyne, be rason
that it is nocht thy facultee to disput in ane profund
mater, the quhilk thy capacite can nocht comprehend ;
therfor i thynk it best that ve recreat our selfis vytht
ioyus comonyng quhil on to the tyme that ve return to
the scheip fald vytht our flokkis : and to begyn sic recreatione i thynk it best that euyrie one of vs tel ane
gude tayl or fabil to pas the tyme quhil 'euyn.' Al the
scheiphirdis, ther vyuis and 'saruandis' var glaid of this
propositione : than the eldest scheiphird began, and al
the laif follouit ane be ane in their 'auen' place." He
then gives the names of the stories and tales he heard,
which are very curious; and thus proceeds : "Quhen

thir scheiphyrdis hed tald al thyr pleysand storeis, than
thay and ther vyuis began to sing sueit melodius sangis
of natural music of the antiquite : the foure marmadyns
that sang quhen Thetis vas mareit on Month Pillion,
thai sang nocht sa sueit as did thir scheiphyrdis, quhilkis
are callit to name Parthenopie, Leucolia, Illigeatempora,
the feyrd callit Legia ; for thir scheiphirdis excedit al
thir four marmadyns in melodius music, in gude accordis
and reportis of dyapason, prolations, and dyatesseron.
The musician 'Amphion,' quhilk sang sa dulce quhil that
the stanis mouit, and alse the scheip and nolt, and the
foulis of the ayr pronuncit there bestial voce to sing
vitht hym ; zit nochtheles, his ermonius sang prefferrit
nocht the sueit sangis of thir foir said scheiphirdis. Nou
i vil reherse sum of the 'sueit' sangis that i herd amang
them as eftir follouis : in the fyrst, 'Pastance vitht gude
companye,'* 'The breir byndis me soir,' 'Stil vnder the
leyuis grene,'† 'Cou thou me the raschis grene,'‡ 'Allace

---

* This is a song by our Henry VIII., as is supposed, of which
the words and music are preserved in a coeval manuscript in the
editor's possession, where it is entitled, "The King's Ballet." It
begins :

> " Passetyme with good cumpanye
> I love, and shall vnto I dye."

† This song is in the Maitland manuscript. It consists of eighteen
stanzas, of which the first is as follows :—

> " Still vndir the levis grene
> This hindir day I went alone,
> I hard ane may sair mwrne and meyne,
> To the king of luif scho maid hir mone :
>   Scho sychtit sely soir,
>   Said, lord, I luif thj loir ;
> Mair wo dreit never woman one,
> O langsum lyfe, and thow war gone,
>   Than sould I mwrne no moir."

‡ See "Ancient Songs," p. 54, (1790.)

i vyit zour tua fayr ene,' 'Gode zou gude day vil boy,'
'Lady help zour presoneir,' 'Kyng Villzamis note,* 'The
lang noune nou,' 'The cheapel-valk,' 'Faytht is there
none,' 'Skald a bellis nou,' 'The Abirdenis nou brume
brume on hil,'† 'Allone i veip in grit distres,' 'Trolee
lolee lemmendou,' 'Bille vil thou cum by a lute and belt
the in sanct Francis cord,' 'The frog cam to the myl
dur,‡ 'The sang of Gilquhiskar,' 'Rycht soirly musing
in my mynde,' 'God sen the duc hed byddin in France
and Delabaute had "neuyr" cum hame,'§ 'Al musing of

---

* This is supposed to be the song sung by Hendy Nicholas in
Chaucer's "Miller's Tale:"

> "And after that he song the kinges note,
> Ful often blessed was his mery throte."

† Here are probably two titles: "Broom, Broom on Hill," at
least, was a popular English ballad. See "Ancient Songs," p. 60,
(1790.)

‡ Mr Warton ("History of English Poetry," vol. iii., p. 445)
says, "There is a ballad, 'A Moste Strange Weddinge of the Frogge
and the Mouse,' licensed by the Stationers to E. White, Nov. 21,
1580." It was doubtless the original of a childish, and, indeed,
nursery song, beginning,

> "There was a frog lived in a well,
> And a farce mouse in a mill," &c.,

which, much altered, and set to a fine Italian air, was a few years
since sung about the streets. See "Gammer Gurton's Garland,"
p. 5, (Stockton, 1784.)

§ John, Duke of Albany, regent during the minority of James V.,
being sent for into France, left in his place Sir Andrew D'Arcy, a
Frenchman, called the Chevalier de la Beaute, who appears to have
been a very gallant and amiable character, and was savagely murdered near Dunbar, by the Laird of Wedderburn and others, in
1517.

meruellis a mys hef i gone,' 'Maestres fayr ze vil forfoyr,'
'O lusty Maye vitht Flora quene,'* 'O myne hart hay

O lust-y May with Fio-ra queen, The balm-y drops from Phe-bus sheen, Pre-lu-sant beams be-fore the day, be-fore the day, the day; By thee Di-a-na grow-eth grecn, Thro' glad-ness of this lust-y May, Thro' glad-ness of this lust-y May.

" Then Aurora that is so bright,
    To woful hearts 'she' casts great light,
    Right pleasantly before the day, &c.
    And shows and sheds furth of that light,
    Through gladness of this lusty May,
    Through gladness of this lusty May.

" Birds on their benghs, of every sort,
    Sends forth their notes, and makes great mirth,
    On banks that blooms on every bray, &c.
    And fares and flyes ov'r field and firth,
    Through gladness, &c.

" All lovers hearts that are in care,
    To their ladies they do repare,
    In fresh mornings before the day, &c.
    And are in mirth ay more and more,
    Through gladness, &c.

" Of every moneth in the year,
    To mirthful May there is no peer ;

this is my sang,' 'The battel of the Hayrlau,'* 'The hunttis of Cheuet,' 'Sal i go vitht zou to Rumbelo fayr,' 'Greuit is my sorrou,'† 'Turne the sueit ville to me,' 'My lufe is lyand seik send hym ioy, send him ioy,' 'Fayr luf lent thou me thy mantil ioy,' 'The Perssee & the Mongumrye met, that day, that gentil day,'‡ 'My luf is laid apon ane knycht,' 'Allace that samyn sueit face,' ' In ane myrthtful morou,' 'My hart is "leinit" on the land.' Thir scheiphirdis ande there vyuis sang mony vther melodius sangis, the quhilkis i hef nocht in memorie : than eftir this sueit celest armonye tha began to dance," &c.

Her glistring garments are so gay,
You lovers all, make merry cheer,
Through gladness of this lusty May,
Through gladness of this lusty May."

A copy of this song, extant in the Hyndford MS., in the Advocates' Library, Edinburgh, contains several variations, and entirely omits the last stanza.

* This is presumed to be the fine poem printed in the " Evergreen," which, with submission to the opinion of the late Lord Hailes, may, for anything that appears, either in or out of it, to the contrary, be as old as the fifteenth century. It does not, at present, give the idea of a song; and must have been sung, if at all, either to a very slow air, or to the common chant. Nothing, perhaps, ought to be inferred unfavourable to the existence of songs not mentioned in this list; and yet one may naturally wonder that it should omit so fine a composition as "Flowden Hili," if then extant.

† See this at full length in "Ancient Songs," p. 93. (1790.) *Greuit* should be *Greuus*.

‡ Two lines of the old original ballad of " Chevy Chase," already named by " The Hunttis of Cheuet." See " Percy's Reliques," &c., vol. i., p. 2. The Scots laid claim to the more modern ballad at an early period, giving themselves the honour of the day, and turning the sarcasm of runaways upon the enemy. They sung it to the tune of "The Yle of Kyle."

That songs in parts were in vogue at this period, we have the direct testimony of Sir David Lindsay, who, in his " Satyre of the Thrie Estaits," (Edin. 1602, 4to,) introduces the character of Solace with these words :—

> " Now quha saw euer sic ane thrang?
> Me thocht sum said I had gaine wrang ;
> Had I help I wald sing ane sang,
>   With ane richt mirrie noyse :
> I haue sic pleasour at my hart,
> That garris me sing THE TROUBILL FAIRT ;
> Wald sum gude fallow fill the quart,
>   It wad my hairt reioyce."

So, again, in another page :—

> " Sister howbeit that I am hais,
> I am content to BEAR A BAIS."

Several " mistoinit sangis" appear to have been sung in the representation of this strange performance ; but nothing of the kind is preserved either in the printed copy or in the manuscript.

The lyric muse would seem of a turbulent disposition, being generally found pretty active in popular disturbances. Even the reformation of religion in this country appears not to have been effected without her assistance. Some time after the king's death, " Ane Wilsoun, servant to the bischope of Dunkeld, quha nether knew the new testament nor the auld, maid a dispyitful railling ballat against the preicheours, and against the governour, for the quilk he narrowly eschaipit hanging :*

---

* " Knox's Historie," p. 33. In another place (p. 77) he preserves the following "sang of triumphe" of the Papists on the surrender of the castle of St Andrews, by those who had slain the archbishop, to the French forces, in 1546; some of the prisoners

the usual method in Scotland of answering a satirical poet.*

In the year 1560, the Protestant party, calling themselves "The congregation of the Lord," headed by James Duke of Chastelherault and others, had taken possession of Edinburgh, where they were already reduced to great straits, when the Count de Martigues arrived from France with a considerable force to the assistance of the Queen-Dowager Regent, and in a very short time after a still more formidable army of English came to that of "The congregation." Many skirmishes happened; the French were besieged in Leith; and the country, no doubt, suffered in every quarter. Of this period is the following song, which, considering the rarity of such like compositions, seems worth preserving :†—

being left in the galleys, "and there," as he says, "miserablie entreatit "—

> "Preistis content yow now, priestis content yow now ;
> For Normond * and his cumpanie hes fillit the gallayis fow."

* See "Crawford's Memoirs," p. 315, (Edinburgh, 1753.)

† In the 4to Maitland MS., whence this is taken, and which is dated 1586, is "Ane ballat to be sunge with the tuine of 'Luifer come to Luifeiris dore,'" &c. It is indifferent and long. In the same MS. is the "Bankis of Helicon," (now published,) in the metre of "The Cherrie and the Slae," and to the tune of which that celebrated poem is, in the Hyndford MS., directed to be sung. See "Ancient Scottish Poems," p. 316, (Edin. 1770;) Tytler's "Dissertation," &c., p. 201. "The Cherrie and the Slae," however, is not in that MS.

N.B.—Since the editor's transcript was made, this ballad has been printed by Pinkerton, ("Ancient Scotish Poems," 1786.)

* Norman Leslie, master of Rothes, one of the prisoners.

" In this new zeir I sie bot weir,
　　Na caus to sing ;
　　In this new zeir I sie bot weir,
　　Na caus thair is to sing.
I can not sing for the vexatioun
Of Frenchmen and the congregatioun,
That has maid trowbill in this natioun,
And monye bair biging.
　　In this new zeir I sie bot weir,
　　Na caus, &c.
　　In this new zeir, &c.

" I haue na will to sing or danse,
　For feir of England and of France :
　God send them sorrow and mischance
　Is caus of their cumming !
　　In this new zeir, &c.

" We ar sa rewlit ritche and puire,
　That we wait not quhair to be suire,
　The Bourdour as the Borrow muire,
　Quhair sum perchance will hing.
　　In this new zeir, &c.

" And zit I think it best that we
　Pluck up our hairt and nirrie be,
　For thocht we wald ly down and die,
　It will ws help na thing.
　　In this new zeir, &c.

" Let ws pray God to stainche this weir,
　That we may leif withouttin feir,
　Inn mirrines quhill we ar heir,
　And hevin at our ending.
　　In this new zeir I sie but weir,
　　Na caus thair is to sing, &c."

Such was the state of Scotish song, when, in the year 1561, Queen Mary returned from France to her native country. No character is to be found in history so nearly approaching excellence and perfection as this illustrious princess, before the turbulence of her unruly and fanatical subjects bewildered her senses, and plunged her into error and misfortune. At any other period, one is almost tempted to say in any other country, such a sovereign would have been the idol of her people.

Not less remarkable for the accomplishments of her mind, than for the beauty of her person, she wrote the most elegant songs, and sang to her lute like an angel.* The only pieces of her composition now known are, it is true, in a foreign tongue, and were written during her happier residence in France, or upon her sorrowful departure from it ;† but it is by no means improbable that she occasionally condescended to honour her mother tongue ; which, barbarous and discordant as it sounded in the delicate ears of the French courtiers, she pronounced with such a grace as to make it appear even to them the most sweet and agreeable. ‡   Yet this princess,

---

* Brantome, " Dames Illustres."

† See a close and elegant version of the beautiful song she composed on her passage in " A Historical Essay on National Song," prefixed to " English Songs," vol. i., for which, as well as for the other poetical translations in that performance, the public is indebted to the late John Baynes, Esq., a gentleman of considerable erudition, uncommon genius, and fine taste, who died universally lamented, at the immature age of twenty-seven.

‡ Brantome, " Dames Illustres." This author, who accompanied the queen to Scotland, gives a curious account of the cordial welcome she met with from her pious and polished subjects :— " Estant logée en bas en l'abbaye de l'Islebourg, vindrent sous la fenestre cinq ou six cents marauts de la ville, luy donner aubade de meschauts violons et petits rebecs, dont il n'y en a faute en ce pays là ; et se mirent à chanter pseaumes, tant mal chantez, et si mal accordez, que rien plus.   He ! quelle musique, et quel repos pour sa nuit."—*Ibi.* These raggamuffins Knox calls "a cumpanie of most honest men," who, he says, " with instruments of musick, and with musicians, gave their salutatiouns at hir chamber window. The melodie," he adds, "as sche alledged, lyked hir weill, and sche willed the same to be continued sum nychts efter with grit diligence."   Her politeness, if the story be true, seems only to have increased the insolence and brutality of this ferocious Reformer and his fanatical adherents.

beautiful, elegant, and accomplished as she was, and
adorned with all the graces that ever centred in woman,
was inhumanly persecuted by barbarous and enthusiastic
ruffians, who owed her allegiance, and had sworn fidelity
to her as their sovereign ; and after nineteen years' con-
finement, was deliberately murdered in cold blood by
an envious, malignant, and treacherous hag, who had
offered her an asylum.*   The injured character of this
illustrious and amiable princess has been completely
vindicated from the calumnies of her malicious accusers,
not in Scotland only, but in England and in France,
within the compass of a few years past.†   Her testament
and letters, which the writer of these pages has seen,
blotted with her tears, in the Scots College, Paris,
will remain perpetual monuments of singular abilities,
tenderness, and affection, of a head and heart, in short,
of which no other queen in the world was probably ever
possessed.

From the manuscript collection of George Bannatyne,
compiled in 1568, Lord Hailes has favoured the public
with a few songs of some value. "The Wowing of Jock
and Jenny" is still popular, and the "Ballat of Evil

---

* It is well known that this execrable fiend tampered with Sir
Amy Powlet and Sir Drue Drury to murder the Queen of Scots
privately, which they had either the virtue or the cunning to
decline.   Her hypocrisy was equal to her cruelty, and she would
have immediately hung them up.   Every one knows how she persecuted Secretary Davison, for despatching the warrant she had
signed for the queen's execution.

† See Goodall's "Examination," &c., 2 vols., (Edin., 1754;)
Tytler's "Inquiry," (Edin., 1760, 1770, 1792 ;) "Histoire d'Elisa-
beth," par Madame Keralio, 5 tomes, (Paris, 1788 ;) and Whit-
aker's "Vindication," &c., 3 vols., (1788, 1790.)

Wyffis," and " Ballat of Guid Fallowis," have no incon-
siderable degree of poetical merit for so remote an age.
" Robene and Makyne," by Henrysone, " The Blait
Luvar," " The Luvaris Lament," by Fethy, and several
pieces by Alexander Scot, though not all, perhaps, properly songs, are entitled to a still higher compliment.
This, indeed, was the Augustan age of Scotish poetry.

James VI., better known as a composer of psalms,
sonnets, and madrigals, is now first mentioned as a
writer of songs. In the library of St Martin's parish,
Westminster, is a MS. volume, containing "all the
king's short poems that are not printed;" and among
these are three songs, the first beginning, "What mortal
man may live but hart;" the second, "When as the
skilful archer false;" the third . . . . being "The first
verses that ever the king made." Whatever may be the
character of these particular pieces, some of his compositions, it ought to be acknowledged, are not destitute of
poetical merit.

" The Bonny Earl of Murray," composed, as it appears, in 1592, may be noticed as a production of this
reign ; as may, likewise, the excellent stanzas of " Tak
yer Auld Cloak about ye," and "Waly, Waly, up the Bank,"
of which the former is directly quoted in Shakespeare's
tragedy of " Othello," supposed to have been written
in 1611; and the other is also cited in a strange but
curious, and apparently antique musical medley published in 1666 : both therefore may be regarded as having been popular songs before the year 1600.*

* The following passages, from others of the like kind in the
same performance, seem also scraps of old songs :—

It was a practice with the pious puritans, as well of England as of Scotland, to write their enthusiastic rhapsodies to the tunes of common and popular songs, of which they generally, if not uniformly, preserved a few lines at the beginning. Of these moralisations, as they are called, a pretty considerable volume was printed, for the second time, at Edinburgh, by Andrew Hart, in the year 1621, under the title of "Ane compendious booke of godly and spirituall songs. Collectit out of sundrie partes of the scripture, with sundrie of other ballates, changed out of prophaine sanges, for avoyding of sinne and harlotrie, with augmentation of sundrie gude and godly ballates, not contained in the first edition. Newlie

---

" Ioly under the green wood tree,
Ioly under the green wood tree,
Be soft and sober, I you pray,
My lady will come here away :
Go graith you in your glansand geer,
To meet my lady pair and pair,
With harps and lutes and guittrons gay,
My lady will come here away.

" Underneath the green wood tree,
There the ' god' Love bideth thee,
    Frisca ioly
Polland the sloe, she doth ago,
    Singing so merrily."

" I saw three ladies fair singing, hey and how upon yon leyland, hey.
I saw three mariners singing Rumbelow, upon yon see stand, hey."

" The pyper's drone was out of tune,
Sing young Thomlin, be merry, be merry, and twise so merry,
With the light of the moon, hey, hey down a down."

" The malt 's come down, be merry, be merry :
The malt 's come down, hey troly loly loly."

" Three birds on a tree,
Three and three, and other three,
The boniest bird come down to me," &c.

corrected and amended by the first originall copie." *
The following are the first stanzas of all the "ballates"
which appear to have been " changed out of prophaine
sanges :"—

> " Richt sorely musing in my minde,
> For pietie sore my herts pynde :

---

* For the sight and use of this singular curiosity, the editor has
to thank Mr George Paton of the Custom House, Edinburgh. It
is a small duodecimo, in black letter. The original impression
must have appeared many years before, as in a MS. " Historie of
the Estate of the Kirke of Scotland, written by ane old minister of
the Kirke of Scotland, at the desire of some of his young brethren
for their informatione," A.D. 1560, in the possession of the same
gentleman, it is said that, "for the more particular meanes whereby
came the knowledge of God's truth in the time of great darkness,
was such as Sir David Lindseye's poesie, Wedderburne's ' Psalmes
and Godlie Ballands,' of godlie purposes," &c. This Wedderburne
was doubtless the identical person who has been already mentioned
as author of the "Complaint of Scotland," 1549; many songs, it is
observable, mentioned in that work being parodied or spiritualised
in this " compendious booke," of which a very injudicious " specimen" was published at Edinburgh by the late Lord Hailes in 1764.
The last article in the book is a poem in three stanzas by King
James I., which it is somewhat extraordinary that Mr Tytler, who
had the perusal of Mr Paton's copy long before he published the
"Poetical Remains " of that monarch, should overlook, unless he
was misled by the note of some former owner of the book to suppose that the words " Quod King James the First " refer generally
to the whole volume, (see "Poetical Remains," &c., p. 32.) It
begins—

> " Sen throw vertue incressis dignity."

It is much to be regretted (*en passant*) that this gentleman should
have been under the necessity of printing the " Kingis Quair" from
a pretended transcript attempted by some illiterate schoolboy, and
abounding, in almost every line, with the most senseless and extravagant blunders, all of which have been religiously preserved in a
subsequent edition printed at Perth.

D

Quhen I remember on Christ so kynde,
    That sauit mee.
Nane culde mee saue from thyle to Ynde
    But onely hee."

" Alace, that same sweit face,
  That deit vpon ane ' tree,'
  To purchase mankynde peace,
  From sinne to make us free,
    Allone to be our remedie."

" Quho is at my windo, who who ?
  Goe from my windo, goe goe :
  Quha calles there, so like ane stranger ?
  Goe from my window, goe :
  Lord, I am here," &c.*

" Intill ane mirthfull May morning,
  Quhen Phebus vp did spring,
  Waking I lay in ane garding gay,
  Thinkand on Christ sa free,
  Quhilk meikly for mankind,
  Tholit to be pynd
    On croce cruelly,   La.   La." †

" All my hart ay this is my sang,
  With doubil mirth and ioy amang ;
  Sa blyth as bird my God to fang,
  Christ hes my hert ay."

" My lufe murnis for me for me,
  My lufe that murnis for me ;
  I am not in kinde hes not in mind
  My lufe that murnis for me."

---

* The original is an English song printed at the end of Hey-
wood's " Rape of Lucrece," (1630,) and, with the music, in D'Urfey's
" Pills to Purge Melancholy," (1719.)   Two stanzas of it are also
quoted in Beaumont and Fletcher's " Knight of the Burning
Pestle."

† The original is as follows :—

    " Into a mirthful May morning,
      As Phebus did up spring,
      I saw a may both fair and gay,
      Most goodly for to see :
      I said to her, Be kind,
      To me that was so pyn'd,
      For your love truly."

" Tell me now and in quhat wise,
　How that I suld my lufe forga.
　Baith day and night ane thousand sise
　　' Thir' tyrannis waikens me with wa."

" Allone I weipe in greit distresse,
　Wee are exilit remedilesse :
　　And wait not why,
　Fra God's word, allace, allace,
　　Uncourteouslie."

" Gryuous is my sorrow,
　Both at euin and morrow,
　Unto myselfe allone :
　Thus Christ makes his mone,
　Saying, Unkindnesse killed mee,
　And puts mee to this paine,
　Allace what remedie,
　For I would not refraine." *

" Johne, cum kis me now,
　Johne, cum kis me now :
　Johne, cum kis me by and by,
　And make no more adow.'

" Musing greitlie in my minde,
　The follie that is in mankinde :
　Whilke is so brukill and so blind,
　And downe sall come, downe aye downe aye.'

" Downe by yond river I ran,
　Downe by yond river I ran,
　Thinkand on Christ sa sweit,
　That broght mee to libertie,
　And I ane sinfull man."

" O Christ quhilk art the light of day,
　The clude of night thou driues away,
　The beame of glore beleuit right,
　Shawand till vs thy perfite light."

" This is na night as naturall,
　Nor zit na clude materiall,
　That thow expels, as I heir say,
　O Christ quhilk art the light of day."

---

* See the original " Ancient Songs," p. 93, (1790.) The parody
contains no fewer than twenty-one stanzas. Another contains
twenty-two, and " Johne, cum kis me now," twenty-six. The rest
contain from four to fifteen.

" With hunts vp, with huntis up,
　　It is now perfite day :
　　Jesus our king is gane in hunting,
　　　Quha likes to speed they may."

" Baneist is faith now euery quhair
　　And sair for thinkes me,
　　Baneist is faith now euery quhair,
　　Be the shauin sort I zow declair,
　　Alace therefore my hert is sair,
　　　And blyth I can noght be."

" The wind blawis cald, furious and bald
　　·This lang and mony day :
　　But Christ's mercy we mon all die,
　　　Or keep the cald wind away.'

" Hay now the day dallis,
　　Now Christ on vs callis,
　　Now welth on our wallis
　　　Appeiris anone :
　　Now the word of God rings,
　　Whilk is king of all kings :
　　Now Christis flock sings,
　　　The night is neere gone."

" Till our gude-man, till our gude-man :
　　Keip faith and loue till our gude-man.
　　For our gude-man in heuin does reigne,
　　In glore and blisse without ending
　　Where angels singes euer Osan,
　　In laude and praise of our gude-man."

" Remember man, remember man,
　　That I thy saull from Sathan wan
　　And hes done for thee what I can,
　　　Thow art full deir formee.
　　Is was, nor sall be none,
　　What may thee saue but I allone,
　　Onely therefore beleiue mee on,
　　　And thou sall neuer die.'

" All * my loue leife me not,
　　Leif mee not, leif mee not,
　　All my loue leif mee not,
　　　Thus mine allone,

---

* *All* is a frequent misprint for *ah ;* probably Hart printed from
on old manuscript copy, in which the *h* had the appearance of *ll*.

With ane burding on my backe,
I may not beir it I am so waik,
Lone, this burding from mee take,
　　Or else I am gone."

There are other pieces in the same volume written apparently in the measure, or to the tune of well-known poems or songs; as, for instance, in one place, "Followis ane sang of the birth of Christ : with the tune of 'Baw lu la law.'"

In Verstegan's "Restitution of Decayed Intelligence," &c., printed originally at Antwerp, in 1605, we meet with the following curious anecdote :—"So fell it out of late years, that an English gentleman travelling in Palestine, not far from Jerusalem, as he passed thorow a country town, he heard by chance a woman sitting at her door dandling her child, to sing, 'Bothwel Bank, thow blumest fayre :' the gentleman hereat exceedingly wondered, and forthwith in English saluted the woman, who joyfully answered him, and said she was right glad there to see a gentleman of our isle, and told him that she was a Scottish woman, and came first from Scotland to Venice, and from Venice thither, where her fortune was to be the wife of an officer under the Turk, who being at that instant absent, and very soon to return, intreated the gentleman to stay there until his return ; the which he did, and she for country sake, to show herself the more kind and bountiful unto him, told her husband, at his homecoming, that the gentleman was her kinsman ; whereupon her husband entertained him very friendly, and at his departure gave him divers things of good value." *　Whatever truth there may be in this

* Edit. 1673, p. 327. In a curious dramatic piece, entitled " Phi

story, no doubt can be entertained as to the existence
of the song, which, it is much to be wished, we were
able to recover. The one containing the same line in a
late publication of " Select Scotish Ballads," vol. ii., is
a despicable forgery.

King Charles I., like his father, was a poet, though
no song writer. His great and gallant general, the
heroic Montrose, has left us some elegant lines, which,
with a few other pieces of this period, will be found
in the present collection.

A sort of music book, printed (for the second time) at
Aberdeen, in 1666, entitled "Cantus : Songs and Fancies,
to three, four, or five parts, both apt for voices and viols.
With a brief introduction to music, as is taught by
Thomas Davidson, in the musick-school of Aberdene,"
is to be mentioned as the first known collection of
Scotish songs, or rather in which Scotish songs are to
be found. These are—"O lusty May with Flora Queen,"
(see before, p. 40;) "Into a mirthful May Morning,"
(see before, p. 50;) "In a Garden so Grene ;" "Come,
Love, let's walk in yonder Spring;" "How should my
feeble body fure ;" "No wonder is suppose my weeping
eyes;" "Like as the dumb solsequium," (by Captain
Montgomery, author of the "Cherrie and the Slae ;")
" The Gowans are gay, my Jo;" "My bailful breast in

lotus," printed at Edinburgh in 1603, by way of finale, is "Ane
Sang of the Foure Lufearis," though little deserving that title. It
is followed by the old English song, beginning—
　　　　" What if a day, or a month, or a year,"
alluded to in "Hudibras," which appears to have been sung at the
end of the play, and was probably at that time new and fashion-
able.

blood all bruist ;" " I love great God above ;" " Where art thou, Hope ;" " Wo worth the Time and eke the Place ;" " Joy to the Person of my Love ;" " Will said to his Mammie ;" " Care, away go thou from me :" two of which, esteemed the best, will be found in the present collection.*

In the Pepysian collection is " a proper new ballad," printed before the Restoration, entitled, " The wind hath blown my Plaid away, or a Discourse betwixt a Young Maid and the Elphin Knight. To be sung with its own pleasant new tune." It contains twenty stanzas, of which the first may serve as a sufficient specimen : —

> " The Elphin knight sits on yon hill,
> Ba, ba, ba, lilli ba,
> He blows his horn both loud and shrill,
> The wind hath blown my plaid awa."

The principal subjects of the dialogue are the knight's proposed condition to have a shirt made without shears, needle, or thread ; and the maid's answer, that he should ear an acre of land with a horn, &c., all which is much better expressed in a little English song, sung by children and nursery maids.†

The restoration of King Charles II., however grateful it might be to a people always strongly attached to their hereditary monarchy, does not appear to have been much celebrated by the muses, nor, violent as were the party convulsions, and numerous and important the events of that reign, has it been found to afford a single song on

---

* It likewise contains the ditty called " What if a day," already mentioned, with the music.

† See Gammer Gurton's " Garland," p. 11.

any historical or political subject. The Whigs, indeed, were addicted solely to prayer and psalm singing, and the Tories too generous, perhaps, to insult so contemptible an adversary, by satirical ballads.

King James VII. was undoubtedly, both before and after his accession, a popular character in Scotland ; and " The 14th of October" (his birth-day) is still a favourite tune. Neither did the imprudence of his religious zeal, which lost him the government of three kingdoms, forfeit the esteem of the people. Averse as they might in general be to his religious tenets, they could not but esteem the lineal descendant of a family which had furnished the country with sovereigns for upwards of a thousand years ; and the justice of whose expulsion was far from manifest. The battle of Killikrankie, fought in 1689, is the subject of a song in the following collection, which may be regarded as the first of the numerous series now called " Jacobite songs."

An inundation of " Scotch songs," so called, appears to have been poured upon the town by Tom D'Urfey, and his Grub Street brethren, toward the end of the last and in the beginning of the present century ; of which, though doubtless highly grateful to the refined taste of the times, it is hard to say whether wretchedness of poetry, ignorance of the Scotish dialect, or nastiness of ideas, is most evident or most despicable. In the number of these miserable caricatures, the reader may be a little surprised to find the favourite songs of " De'ill take the War that hurry'd Willy from me ;" " O Jenny, Jenny, where hast thou been ?" " Young Philander woo'd me lang ;" " Farewell my bonny, witty, pretty

Moggy;" "In January last;" "She rose and let me in;" "Pretty Kate of Edinburgh;" "As I sat at my Spinning-wheel;" "Fife and a' the Lands about it;" "Bonny Lad, prithee lay thy Pipe down;" "The bonny grey-eyed Morn;" "'Twas within a Furlong of Edinburgh Town;" "Bonny Dundee;" "O'er the Hills and far away;" "By Moonlight on the Green;" "What's that to you?" and several others, which he has been probably used to consider as genuine specimens of Scotish song; as indeed most of them are regarded even in Scotland.*

The insurrection, in 1715, of the adherents to the person whom his friends called James VIII., and his enemies the pretender, but who, in any case, was the legitimate son of King James VII., seems to have roused the poetic even more than the military spirit of the Scots. Many songs were composed on this event, of which some of those which have been preserved will not be found destitute of merit.

In the year 1719, the celebrated poem or ballad of

---

* See D'Urfey's "Pills to Purge Melancholy," *passim*. In vol. iv. is "A Scotch Song. The words by Mr John Hallam. Set to music by Mr John Cottrell," beginning, "Upon the wings of love, my dear, I come;" and in the next volume is another, "the words by Mr Peter Noble; set by Mr John Wilford," beginning "Bonny Scottish lads that keens me weel."

"She rose and let me in," however, ought not to be confounded with the rest, as it is an English song of great merit, and has been Scotified by the Scots themselves. The modern air, a fine composition, (probably by Oswald,) is very different from that in the "Pills." "De'ill take the Wars," written by D'Urfey, and sung in "A Wife for any Man," Mr Tytler classes in his "third æra,— from Queen Mary to the Restoration."

" Hardyknute" first appeared, at Edinburgh, as a " fragment," in a folio pamphlet of twelve pages.   That it is
of no greater antiquity must be perfectly clear, from
every species of evidence, intrinsic or extrinsic, and
the only means of reconciling the seemingly opposite
accounts of its birth, is to conclude it the illegitimate
offspring of Mrs Wardlaw, by Sir John Bruce.*   The
two stanzas beginning, " Aryse, zoung knicht," the three
beginning, " Now with his ferss and stalwart train," the
two beginning, " Sair bleids my leige," the six beginning,
" Quhair lyke a fyre," and the three last, are not in the
first edition, (which was reprinted in four leaves, 8vo,)
but originally appeared in the " Ever Green," in which
many different readings are given, and Ramsay, to confirm the authenticity of the whole, has everywhere changed
the initial *y* to *z*.   That a composition abounding with
evident imitations of, and direct allusions to modern and
familiar poetry,† in short, that a palpable and bungling

---

* The former pretended to have found it written on "the bottoms
of clues," the other "in a vault at Dumfermline."   See Dr Percy's
" Reliques," &c., vol. ii., pp. 96, 111; " Ancient Scotish Poems,"
vol. i., p. 127.   Mr Thomson, the Scotish musician, finding the
cause to stick, as the Turks say, or, in other words, the tide of suspicion running very strong against it, declared, like a hardy Scot,
that " he had heard fragments of it repeated during his infancy,
before ever Mrs Wardlaw's copy was heard of," though there is
not a single line, not stolen from some old ballad, that has the
most distant appearance of having existed before.   The evidence of
Ossian's witnesses is exactly like that of Mr Thomson.

    † " Drinking the blude-reid wine."—Stan. 5, l. 8.
      " Drinking the blude-reid wine."—Sir Patrick Spence.
      " Full twenty thousand *glittering* spears."—Stan. 6, l. 3.
      " Full twenty thousand *Scottish* spears."—*Chevy Chase.*

forgery, without the slightest resemblance of anything ancient or original, should have passed, either in England or Scotland, for a genuine relique of antiquity, would appear almost incredible and miraculous, if there were not subsequent instances of a similar delusion. Why the Scotish literati should be more particularly addicted to literary imposition than those of any other country, might be a curious subject of investigation for their new Royal Society. Dr Johnson, indeed, is of opinion that "a Scotchman must be a very sturdy moralist, who does not love Scotland better than truth ; he will always love it," he says, "better than inquiry; and if falsehood flatters his vanity, will not be very diligent to detect it." He is speaking of another forgery—the

> " Then furth he drew his trusty glaive,
>   Quhyle thousands all around,
>   Drawn frae their sheaths, glanst in the sun."—Stan. 21.

> " He spake : and to confirm his words outflew
>   Millions of flaming swords, drawn from the thighs
>   Of mighty cherubim ; the sudden blaze
>   Far round illumin'd hell."—MILTON.

The author, either through ignorance or from affectation, uses *Britain* and *Britons* as synonymous with *England* and *English ;* and the editor of " Scotish Tragic Ballads," (1781,) has had the impudence to assert, that " this [last] was the common name which the Scots gave the English anciently, as may be observed in their old poets; and particularly ' Blind Harry :'" though the " Life of Wallace" is a common book, in which the word *Britons* is not to be found.

Mr Tytler, however, seems to consider " Hardyknute" as authentic. " All our old heroic ballads," says he, " such as ' Hardiknute,' and others, were *undoubtedly* sung to *chants* composed for them, which are now lost." The truth, indeed, seems too well ascertained to admit of a *doubt ;* the Scotish critics should recollect an excellent old maxim—" *De non apparentibus et de non existentibus eadem est ratio.*"

poems of Ossian. However this may be, the fact is incontestable; and the forgeries of Hector Boethius, David Chalmers, George Buchanan, Thomas Dempster, Sir John Bruce, William Lauder, Archibald Bower, James Macpherson, and John Pinkerton, stamp a disgrace upon the national character, which ages of exceptionless integrity will be required to remove; an era, however, which, if one may judge from the detestation in which the most infamous and despicable of these impostors is universally held, has already commenced.

In the year 1724, Allan Ramsay, a barber in Edinburgh, first published "The Tea-table Miscellany; or, A Collection of Choice Songs, Scots and English;" to which we are indebted for the preservation of several old Scotish songs of great merit, of which no earlier copies are now to be found, as well as for many excellent originals written, as it seems, either by himself or others, purposely for this publication. Ramsay was a man of strong natural parts, and a fine poetical genius, of which his celebrated pastoral, "The Gentle Shepherd," will ever remain a substantial monument; and though some of his songs may be deformed by far-fetched allusions and pitiful conceits, "The Lass of Peattie's Mill," "The Yellow-Hair'd Laddie," "Farewell to Lochaber," and some others, must be allowed equal to any, and even superior, in point of pastoral simplicity, to most lyric productions, either in the Scotish or any other language.* As an editor, he is, per-

---

* It is somewhat strange that Mr Tytler, knowing both when Ramsay began to write, and the songs of which he is the author, should consider several of his undoubted compositions among the

haps, reprehensible, not only on account of the liberties
he appears to have taken with many of the earlier pieces
he published, in printing them with additions,* which
one is unable to distinguish, but also for preferring
songs written by himself, or the "ingenious young gentlemen" who assisted him, to ancient and original words,
which would, in many cases, all circumstances considered, have been probably superior, or, at least, much
more curious, and which are now irretrievable.† In

fine songs which "we may almost with certainty pronounce to have
been made" within his "last æra—that is, from the Restoration to
the Union.'

* He marks the following pieces with the letter Z as "old
songs:"—"Muirland Willie," "Scornfu' Nancy," "Maggie's
Tocher," "For the Love of Jean," "The Blythsome Bridal," "Fint
a Crum of Thee she faws," "The Auld Goodman," "The Shepherd
Adonis," "John Ochiltree," "In January last," "General Lesly's
March," "The Deceiver," (English,) "Todlen But, and todlen Ben,"
"Rob's Jock," "Country Lass," "Waly, waly," "O'er the Hills and
far away," "Norland Jocky and Southland Jenny;" the following
with Q as "old songs, with additions:"—"Lucky Nancy," "Auld
Rob Marris," "Ew Bughts Marrion," "*Omnia vincit amor*," "The
Auld Wife beyont the Fire," "Sleepy Body," "Jocky, blyth and
gay," "Had away from me, Donald," "The Peremptory Lover,"*
"What's that to you?" "Jocky fou, Jenny fain," "Jenny, where
has' thou been?" Some indisputably old songs, however, are printed
without either of these letters.

† Every reader of taste or sentiment will regret that he should
have preferred his own trifling stanzas to the original of a song
founded on the following anecdote:—"The celebrated 'Bessie Bell
and Mary Gray' are buried near Lednoch. The common tradition
is, that the father of the former was laird of Kinvaid, in the neigh-
bourhood of Lednoch, and the father of the latter laird of Lednoch;

* The enlargement of this song seems to have been intrusted to one of his
Irish journeymen, the *additions* consisting in the *omission* of three whole
stanzas.

short, Ramsay would seem to have had too high an opinion of his own poetry, to be a diligent or faithful publisher of any other person's.*   Among the contribu-

that these two young ladies were both very handsome, [and] a most intimate friendship subsisted between them ; that while Miss Bell was on a visit to Miss Gray the plague broke out, in the year 1666, in order to avoid which they built themselves a bower, about three-quarters of a mile west from Lednoch House, in a very retired and romantic place, called Burn Braes, on the side of Brauchie Burn. Here they lived for some time, but the plague raging with great fury, they caught the infection, it is said, from a young gentleman who was in love with them both, and here they died.   The burial-place lies about half a mile west from the present house of Led-noch," ("Muses' Threnodie," p. 19, 1774.) The first four, or per-haps eight, lines of Ramsay's song are supposed to be taken from the original, with which it seems to be confounded by Mr Pennant, ("Tour in Scotland in 1772,") part ii., p. 112)—

> " O Bessy Bell and Mary Gray,
>   They are twa bonny lasses,
>   They bigg'd a bower on yon burn-brae,
>   And theek'd it o'er wi' rashes.
>   Fair Bessy Bell I loo'd yestreen,
>   And thought I ne'er cou'd alter,
>   But Mary Gray's twa pawky een,
>   They gar my fancy falter."

We should likewise have been much more indebted to him for the insertion of the elegant ballad of "Gilderoy," than of an English song, beautiful as it may be, to the same tune. If Sir Alexander Halket were actually the author of this ballad, its age may be pro-bably ascertained ; it was certainly written before the present cen-tury.   Mr Tytler says it was made on the death of a famous outlaw hanged by James V., an assertion, however, which it expressly contradicts. He appears, in fact, from Spalding's account, to have been a sort of chief or leader of the proscribed Clan Gregor, and, "with five other lymmars," to have been hanged at Edinburgh in the month of July 1636.

* He is, however, very inconsistently censured by a late writer, who has stuffed two despicable volumes of what he is pleased to call "the very best of Scotish ballad poetry," not only with the

tors to this collection, which, except the musical publication at Aberdeen, is supposed to be the first that ever
appeared of Scotish songs,* was a gentleman of the name
of Crawford, of the family of Auchnames; whom the
pastoral beauties and elegant language of "Tweedside,"
and the pathetic tenderness of "My Deary, an ye die,"
will ever place in the first rank of lyric poets.† In this
list we also find Mr Hamilton of Bangour, an elegant
writer, whose "Braes of Yarrow" will be long admired,‡
and Mr Mallet, (then Malloch,) to whom we owe two

most infamous forgery, (of which Ramsay cannot be accused,) but
with a variety of his own unnatural productions, compared to which
the bathos of Ramsay is perfect sublimity—

"Thou write pindaricks, and be damn'd!"

* A few are printed, but very incorrectly, in "A Collection of
Scots Poems," 1706, &c.

† The editor confesses that the omission of "Down the Burn,
Davie," (which Mr Tytler has *conjectured* a composition of the
space of time "from Queen Mary to the Restoration," as he has
done other songs of this gentleman to have been made within his
"last æra—from the Restoration to the Union,") though inten-
tional, has not been without regret.

‡ Dr Percy ("Reliques of Ancient English Poetry," vol. ii., p.
371, 1775) observes, that "The Braes of Yarrow" was written in
imitation of an old Scotish ballad on a similar subject, with the
same burden to each stanza. The author, indeed, expressly avows
it to be "in imitation of the ancient Scotish manner;" but both
these assertions have been doubted. Mr Tytler, however, mentions
"Busk ye, busk ye, my bonny Bride," among the songs and tragic
ballads within his *second epoch,*—that is, "from the beginning of
the reign of King James IV., James V., and to the end of that of
Queen Mary"—which, to those who never heard of any other ballad of this description than that by Mr Hamilton, who died in
1754, will appear somewhat extraordinary. It is not, however,
always easy to know when Mr Tytler is speaking of the words, and
when he means only the melodies of the songs he mentions. There

beautiful stanzas, " The Shades of Endermay," and one
of the finest ballads that ever were written.*

Joseph Mitchell, who died in 1738, may be mentioned
as a song writer of very inferior merit ; none of his compositions deserving to be rescued from oblivion.   The
beautiful pastoral of " Robin and Nanny," by Lord Bin-
ning, will cause every reader to regret that it is the only
song of that promising young nobleman's composition
known to be extant.

The gallant attempt made by a delicate young prince
to recover the throne of his ancestors, in 1745, seems to
have been hailed by the Scotish muse with her most

are, indeed, a few stanzas preserved of a ballad " to the tune of
' Leader Haughs and Yarrow,' " which have some merit, although
its origin or antiquity cannot be ascertained.

> " I dream'd a dreary dream last light—
>   God keep us a' frae sorrow !
> I dream'd I pu'd the birk sae green
>   Wi' my true luve on Yarrow.
>
> " ' I 'll read your dream, my sister dear,
>   I 'll tell you a' your sorrow :
> You pu'd the birk wi' your true luve ;
>   He 's kill'd, he 's kill'd on Yarrow.'
>
> " O gentle wind, that bloweth south
>   To where my love repaireth,
> Convey a kiss from his dear mouth,
>   And tell me how he fareth !
>
> ' But o'er yon glen run arm'd men,
>   Have wrought me dule and sorrow;
> They 've slain, they 've slain the comliest swain :
>   He bleeding lies in Yarrow."

* Ramsay, at the end of a separate edition of " William and
Margaret," observes, " This ballad will sing to the tunes of " Montrose's Lines," " Rothe's Lament," or " The Isle of Kell ;" and
yet Thomson, not above three years after, publishes it as " an *old*
Scotch ballad with the *original* Scotch tune."

brilliant strains. On no occasion did ever such a multitude of songs appear, of which several are among the finest specimens of lyrical composition. "The Tears of Scotland," in particular, by Dr Smollett, is, for pathetic sentiment and elegant versification, certainly not excelled by anything that ever was, or ever will be, written in any language whatever. An ode, likewise, by Mr Hamilton of Bangour, on the victory at Gladsmuir, has great poetical merit. Neither of these poems, however, though both have been set to music, seems in strictness to fall within the description of a song, as they belong, in fact, to a superior class of poetry. A few select pieces will be found in the present collection; but it is believed that numbers of equal or superior merit have either perished, or are not now to be met with in print.* To offer any apology for the republication of these political effusions would be to insult those who might be suspected to require it. The rival claims of Stewart and Brunswick are not more to the present generation than those of Bruce and Baliol, or York and Lancaster. The question of RIGHT has been submitted to the arbitration of the SWORD, and is now irrevocably decided; but neither that decision, nor any other motive, should deter the historian from doing justice to the character of those brave men who fell in a cause which they, at least,

* The editor has heard a few lines of a fine parody of "Rule Britannia," of which he could never obtain a copy. The chorus ran thus—

"Rise, Britannia, Britannia, rise and fight!
Restore your injured monarch's right."

The original words seem to have been inserted in the "Loyal Songs" (1750) by mistake.

E

thought right, and which others, perhaps, only think wrong, as it proved unsuccessful.*

Robertson of Struan, who died aged in 1749, ought to be regarded as the poet of an earlier period. The few songs he has left, though far unequal to his beautiful and pathetic elegies, are by no means destitute of merit.†
Smollett, who has been already mentioned, is the author of two most elegant songs. The few written by Thomson would, perhaps, have done greater credit to a genius of less magnitude, but are by no means unworthy of him.
Mallet, too, who new wrote the masque of " Alfred," which was originally the joint composition of himself and Thomson, has enriched his alteration with a few songs that might have procured celebrity to any but the author of " William and Margaret."

Alexander Ross, author of the " Fortunate Shepherdess," and living at the time of its publication in 1768, must have been very aged, if the tune of " A Rock and a Wee Pickle Tow," mentioned by Ramsay, allude to the song he then printed. The only fault of this humorous performance is its great length, which has

---

* It is judiciously observed by the patriotic Fletcher, that "as the most just and honourable enterprises, when they fail, are accounted in the number of rebellions, so all attempts, however unjust, if they succeed, always purge themselves of all guilt and imputation"—an observation which might be sufficiently illustrated by English history. It had been already made, indeed, by Sir John Harington—

> " Treason does never prosper. What's the reason?
> For if it prosper none dare call it treason."

† There are several ascribed to him in the " Scots Musical Museum," which are not in his " Poems," (1749.) He is also said to have composed a great many in the Erse language.

induced former editors to retrench no fewer than fourteen stanzas ; unless, indeed, they were added after the original publication.   The dialect he uses is broad Buchans, which considerably heightens the ludicrous turn of his composition.

The history of Scotish poetry exhibits a series of fraud, forgery, and imposture, practised with impunity and success.   The ballad of "Gil Morrice" was printed, for the second time, at Glasgow, in 1755, with an advertisement, setting forth, "that its preservation was owing to a lady, who favoured the printers with a copy, as it was carefully collected from the mouths of old women and nurses ;" and "any reader that can render it more correct or complete," is desired to oblige the public with such improvements.   In consequence of this advertisement, as we learn from Dr Percy, no less than sixteen additional verses were produced and handed about in manuscript, which that editor, though he conjectures them after all to be only an ingenious interpolation, has inserted in their proper places.   These are, he says, from verse 109 to 121, and from verse 124 to 129.*   The doctor assures us, that in his ancient folio MS. "is a very old imperfect copy of the same ballad : wherein, though the leading features of the story are the same, yet the colouring here is so much improved and heightened, and so many additional strokes are thrown in, that it is evident the whole has undergone a revisal."   This MS., we are told, instead of "Lord Barnard," has "John

* It should seem from this as if the learned prelate had been satisfied of the authenticity of the three last stanzas, which bear the strongest possible marks of illegitimacy.

Stewart," and instead of " Gil Morrice," " Child Maurice, which last is probably the original title." This " little pathetic tale" is said to have " suggested the plot of the tragedy of ' Douglas ;'" and Dr Percy " had been assured that the ballad is still current in many parts of Scotland, where the hero is universally known by the name of Child Maurice, pronounced by the common people Cheild or Cheeld ; which," says he, " occasioned the mistake." The original stanzas, even as the ballad is now printed, may be easily distinguished from the interpolations ; great part of the latter being a more evident and pitiful forgery than " Hardyknute," which, with another modern production, the interpolator has had the folly or impudence to imitate or transcribe.*

* " The baron he is a man of might,
  He neir could bide to taunt,
  As ze will see before its nicht
   How sma' ze hae to vaunt."—Stan. 6.

" Aft Britain's blude has dimd its shyne,
  This poynt cut short their vaunt,
  Syne pierced the boister's bairded cheik,
   Nae tyme he tuek to taunt."—*Hardyknute.*

" The boy was clad in robes of green."—Stan. 15.

" The boy put on his robes, his robes of green."—*Braes of Yarrow.*

" And like the mavis on the bush,
  He gart the vallies ring."—Stan. 15.

" I sang, my voice the woods returning."—*Braes of Yarrow.*

" He sang so sweet it might dispel
  A' rage but fell despair."—Stan. 16.

" Vernal delight and joy : able to drive
  All sadness but despair."—Milton.

" Obraid me not, my lord Barnard !
  Obraid me not for shame."—Stan. 23.

" My brother Douglas may upbraid."—*Braes of Yarrow.*

The merit of Dr Blacklock's song, "The Braes of Ballendine," is considerably enhanced by the circumstance under which it was composed—a total privation of sight. Mr Falconer, the ingenious and unfortunate author of that excellent descriptive poem, "The Shipwreck," has left a pretty song, which will be found in the present collection; another, it was thought less necessary to insert, occurs in the "St James's Magazine"

.

> " To me nae after days nor nichts
>   Will eir be saft or kind."—*Stan.* 24.

> " To me nae after day nor nicht
>   Can eir be sweit or fair."—*Hardyknute.*

> " With waefou wae I heard zour plaint."—*Stan.* 25, l. 1.

> " Quhat wae fou wae her bewtie bred."—*Hardyknute.*

> " Had gard his body bleid."—*Stan.* 25, l. 4.

> " He gard his body bleid."—*Hardyknute.*

> " Dry up zour tears, my winsom dame,
>   Ye neir can heal the wound."—*Stan.* 25.

> " Return and dry thy useless sorrow;
>   Busk ye, busk ye, my winsome marrow."—*Braes of Yarrow.*

> " Ye see his head upon the spear,
>   His heart's blude on the ground."—*Stan.* 25.

> " My luver's blude is on thy speir."—*Braes of Yarrow.*

> " I curse the hand that did the deid," &c.—*Stan.* 26.

> " Curse ye, curse ye, his useless useless shield,
>   My arm that wrought the deid of sorrow," &c.—*Braes of Yarrow.*

> " The comely zouth to kill."—*Stan.* 26, l. 4.

> " 'Tis he the comely swain I slew."—*Braes of Yarrow.*

Many lines, and indeed entire stanzas, of this ballad occur also in two inedited ones, entitled "Jack, the Little Scot," and "Lady Maisery."

for October 1762, and is there said to be "written at
sea." The first stanza is as follows :—

> " A nymph of every charm possess'd
>   That native virtue gives,
> Within my bosom all confess'd,
>   In bright idea lives.
> For her my trembling numbers play
>   Along the pathless deep,
> While sadly social with my lay
>   The winds in concert weep."

Mr Home, author of the tragedy of "Douglas," is also
to be numbered in the list of Scotish song writers ; but
it must be confessed that "The Banks of the Dee"* has
lost much of its popularity, though surely nothing of its
merit, since the "valiant Jemmy" failed to "quell the
proud rebels." That Jemmy's ghost now wanders on
those banks, instead of his person, might be no improper or unpathetic subject for a second part.

Dr Alexander Webster is to be noticed as the author
of a song of much merit, beginning—

> " O how shall I venture to love one like thee?"

A collection (by Mr D. Herd) was published at Edinburgh in 1769, under the title of "The Ancient and
Modern Scots Songs, Heroic Ballads, &c., now collected
into one body, from the various miscellanies wherein
they formerly lay dispersed;" of which a second edition, in two volumes, appeared in 1776. To this, though

---

* This song being written to the Irish air of "Langolee," a late
writer says that "such a theft cannot be too severely condemned,
as if persisted in there is an end of all national music"—an opinion
which must be allowed to come with peculiar propriety from one
who has been guilty of every species of forgery and imposition.
There is no theft in the case; and to accuse an air of impurity is
completely absurd.

not so judiciously selected or arranged as it might have
been, and containing many confessedly English songs, a
few supposititious ballads, and several pieces unworthy
of preservation, we are certainly indebted for a number
of excellent and genuine compositions never before
printed, as the editor of the present collection is bound
in gratitude to acknowledge.

Robert Fergusson, who died in 1774, is the author of
two tolerably pretty love songs, which may be found
among his poems. Robert Burns, a natural poet of the
first eminence, does not, perhaps, appear to his usual
advantage in song—*non omnia possumus*. The political
"fragment," as he calls it, inserted in the second volume
of the present collection, has, however, much merit in
some of the satirical stanzas, and could it have been
concluded with the spirit with which it is commenced,
would indisputably have been entitled to great praise;
but the character of his favourite minister seems to have
operated like the touch of a torpedo; and after vainly
attempting something like a panegyric, he seems under
the necessity of relinquishing the task. Possibly the
bard will one day see occasion to complete his performance as a uniform satire.*

Messrs Picken, Galloway, Fisher, and Shirrefs, each of
whom has published a volume of his poetical works, are
to be numbered among the writers of Scotish songs;

---

* Mr Burns, as good a poet as Ramsay, is, it must be regretted,
an equally licentious and unfaithful publisher of the performances of
others. Many of the original, old, ancient, genuine songs inserted
in Johnson's "Scots Musical Museum" derive not a little of their
merit from passing through the hands of this very ingenious critic.

and others, perhaps, of equal celebrity, might be found, if necessary, to increase the list.

The public curiosity was a good deal excited by the publication of a volume of " Scottish tragic ballads," as they are called, in 1781 ; the performance, it appeared, of Mr John Pinkerton, who had already rendered himself pretty remarkable by some very extraordinary poetical rhapsodies, now deservedly forgotten.   This volume was ushered in with two " dissertations," in which there is a strange jumble of all sorts of reading, and a variety of extravagant assertion, very little, it must be confessed, to the purpose of the work in hand, or, indeed, to any other.   The most prominent feature in this little volume is the studied and systematic forgery that pervades the whole.   " The mutilated fragment of ' Hardyknute,' " of which a second part now first saw the light, and both clothed in affectedly antique orthography, is said to be " given in its original perfection," and, with equal truth and modesty, pronounced " the most noble production in this style that ever appeared in the world :" the editor professing himself " indebted for most of the stanzas now recovered, to the memory of a lady in Lanarkshire ;" and asserting that the common people of that province could " repeat scraps of both parts."   " A few other monuments of ancient Scottish poetry," he adds, " are now first published from tradition."   These are, " The Laird of Woodhouselie," " Lord Livingston," " Binnorie," " The Death of Menteith," and " I wish I were where Helen lies :" of the forgery of which pieces, as well as of the second part of " Hardyknute," and two pretended fragments, the author, in a subsequent publication, (but not

till he had been directly accused by a letter in the
" Gentleman's Magazine,"*) confessed himself guilty.
" This man," is what the courtesy of the age calls a
gentleman, and yet, to borrow his own words, "if he
had used the same freedom in a private business which
he has in poetry, he would have been set on the pil-
lory :" † and, in fact, "to call such an infamous impostor by his very worst but true title, were but justice to
society." ‡

It is remarkable that some of the finest lyric compositions of Scotland have been produced by the fair sex.
Lady Grissel Baillie is the author of a pathetic ballad,
which is said by an eminent and judicious writer to be
" executed with equal truth and strength of colouring."
Few songs in any language are equal to the " Flowers of

---

* For November 1784. Had this letter (upon which the editor
of that work, out of his singular *urbanity*, allowed the culprit the
extraordinary privilege of making false and evasive comments previous to its publication) never appeared, these contemptible forgeries
would have continued to disgrace the annals of Scotish poetry, till
at least the pretence of antiquity had proved too slight a buoy to
support the weight of their intrinsic dulness.

† "Enquiry," &c., vol. i. p. 241.

‡ "Ancient Scotish Poems," vol. i. p. ci., (1786.) Of this
shocking propensity to forgery and falsehood, (for every imposition
has a lie or two in its support,) he gave reiterated proofs in a second
volume of "Comic Ballads," published along with a new edition of
the first in 1783. In palliation of his crime, in the true spirit of a
"last dying speech," he pleads his youth and purity of intention,
professing that "the imposition was only to give pleasure to the
public." For "as to the vanity," adds he, "or pleasure of impos-
ing upon others, if there be such ideas, they are quite unknown to
the editor"—all which, it is to be hoped, he has found some chari-
table person disposed to believe.

Yarrow," by Miss Home ;* while the elegant and accomplished authoress of "Auld Robin Gray" has, in this beautiful production, to all that tenderness and simplicity for which the Scotish song has been so much celebrated, united a delicacy of expression which it never before attained.† We may, therefore, conclude that this species of composition, which has been carried to the utmost perfection, must either cease or degenerate.

Though the merit of the Scotish songs is generally allowed, it cannot be pretended that they possess any uniformity of excellence. Such as have been composed

---

* If it be to this lady (now Mrs Hunter) that we are also indebted for "The Death-Song of the Cherokee Indian," one can scarcely tell whether to admire most the genius that could produce two such masterly and opposite compositions, or the indifference which occasions this note.

† The writer, of whom so much notice has been already taken, after observing that none of the "Scotch amatory ballads," as he remembers, "are written by ladies," and that the "profligacy of manners which always reigns before women can so utterly forget all sense of decency and propriety as to commence authors, is yet almost unknown in Scotland," adds, in a note, that "there is, indeed, of very late years one insignificant exception to this rule: 'Auld Robin Gray,' having got his silly psalm set to soporific music, is, to the credit of our taste, popular for the day; but, after lulling some good-natured audiences asleep, he will soon fall asleep himself." Alas! this "silly psalm" will continue to be sung, "to the credit of our taste," long after the author of this equally ridiculous and malignant paragraph (whose most virulent censure is indeed the highest praise) shall be as completely forgotten as yesterday's ephemeron, and his printed trash be only occasionally discernible at the bottom of a pie. Of the twenty-four Scotish song-writers whose names are preserved, four, if not five, are females, and, as poetesses, two more might be added to the number.

by persons of education, conversant with the poetry of other countries, though occasionally superior, will more frequently be found inferior, to English compositions. We have many songs equal, no doubt, to the best of those written by Hamilton of Bangour, or Mr Thomson; though it may be questioned whether any English writer has produced so fine a ballad as "William and Margaret," or such a beautiful pastoral as "Tweedside." The truth is, that there is more of art than of nature in the English songs; at all events, they possess very little of that pastoral simplicity for which the Scotish are so much admired, and which will be frequently found to give them the advantages which the beautiful peasant, in her homespun russet, has over the fine town lady, patched, powdered, and dressed out for the ball or opera in all the frippery of fashion.

One cannot, however, adduce the performance of scholars and distinguished individuals as specimens of national song. The genuine and peculiar natural song of Scotland is to be sought, not in the works of Hamilton, Thomson, Smollett, or even Ramsay, but in the productions of obscure or anonymous authors, of shepherds and milk-maids, who actually felt the sensations they describe—of those, in short, who were destitute of all the advantages of science and education, and perhaps incapable of committing the pure inspirations of nature to writing;* and in this point of view, it is be-

---

* That songs have been composed by fiddlers, we have the express testimony of Allan Ramsay, in his "Elegy on Patie Birnie," where he says—

> " Your honour's father dead and gane,
> For him he first wa'd make his mane ;

lieved, the English have nothing equal in merit, nor in fact anything of the kind. The songs to which one may refer as proofs of this position, and give as specimens of the native song of Scotland, are—" Ewbughts Marrion," " The Lowlands of Holland," " Etrick Banks," " Flowden Hill," " The Silken-snooded Lassie," " Here awa', there awa'," " My Heart's my Ain," " As I was a-Walking ae May Morning," " Sweet Annie fra the Sea-beach came," " Willy's rare," " Waly, waly," " Cock Laird," " My Joe Janet," " Hooly and Fairly," " Get Up and Bar the Door," " Maggie's Tocher," " Muirland Willie," and others of the like kind, of which numbers, it is believed, have never been collected, or perhaps never written. The irregular style and pathetic simplicity of one species, and the ludicrous gaiety of the other, are equally natural and interesting ; and though many imitations of these peculiarities, by writers of a different description, have been very happy and successful, they are not the less characteristic of the originals, which abound with touches of nature and simplicity not to be paralleled in more laboured or regular productions.

> But soon his face cou'd make ye fain
> When he did sough—
> 'O wiltu, wiltu do 't again?'
> And gran'd and leugh.

> "'This sang he made fra his ain head,
> And eke, "The auld man's mare she's dead,
> Though peats and tures and a's to lead :"
> O fy upon her !
> A bonny auld thing this indeed,
> An't like yer honour.

" He boasted," according to the note, " of being a poet as well as a musician." This latter song, however, has been ascribed in print to a Mr Watt.

There are in Scotland many ballads, or legendary and romantic songs, composed in a singular style, and preserved by tradition among the country people ; some of these* will be found inserted in Mr Herd's collection of " Scots Songs;" and for a collection of others,† not hitherto published, the editor of these volumes is indebted to the liberality and politeness of Alexander Fraser Tytler, Esq. It must, however, be confessed, that none of these compositions bear satisfactory marks of the antiquity they pretend to, while the expressions or allusions occurring in some would seem to fix their origin to a very modern date. But, in fact, with respect to vulgar poetry preserved by tradition, it is almost impossible to discriminate the ancient from the modern, the true from the false. Obsolete phrases will be perpetually changing for those better understood ; and what the memory loses the invention must supply. So that a performance of genius and merit, as the purest stream becomes polluted by the foulness of its channel, may in time be degraded to the vilest jargon. Tradition, in

---

* " Bothwell," " Fine Flowers o' the Valley," " Lizie Wan," " May Colvin," " The Wee, Wee Man," " Sir Hugh," and " The Jew's Daughter," (different copies,) " Earl Douglas," (a fragment,) " Lammikin," " The Bonny Lass of Lochroyan," " Kertonha'," " Clerk Colvill," " Willie and Annet," " The Cruel Knight," " Wha will Bake my Bridal Bread ?" " Lizae Baillie," " Good Morrow, fair Mistress," " Duncan," and " Kenneth," are clearly supposititious.

† These are—" Willie's Lady," " Clark Colven," (a different copy,) " Brown Adam," " Jack the Little Scot," " Chil' Brenton," " The Gay Gosshawk," " Young Bekie," " Rose the Red and White Lillie," " Brown Robin," " Willie o'," " Douglass Dale," " Kempion," " Lady Elspat," " King Henry," " Lady Maisery," and " The Cruel Sister."

short, is a species of alchemy which converts gold to lead. The most favourable specimens of this species of old Scotish ballad are probably—"Willie and Annet," "The Cruel Knight," and the two fragments, "Wha will Bake my Bridal Bread?" and "Good Morrow, fair Mistress, the beginner of strife." Few of the others will bear publication, being rather remarkable by a sort of wild whimsical puerility of idea, barrenness of language, and neglect of rhyme—by a total want, in short, of everything for which poetry, even of the vulgarest kind, is entitled to admiration or allowance. He, however, who should have the patience to collect, the judgment to arrange, and the integrity to publish the best pieces of this description, would probably deserve the thanks of the antiquary and the man of taste ; but would more probably excite the malicious attacks and scurrilous language of a few despicable hirelings, who, to the disgrace of criticism, of letters, and liberality, are permitted to dictate their crude and superficial ideas as the criterion of literary eminence. There is one song, or rather the fragment of one, which seems to merit particular attention from a singular evidence of its origin and antiquity: it is inserted in the present collection, under the title or "The Wee, Wee Man," and begins—

" As I was walking all alone."

The original of this song is extant in a Scotish or North-umbrian poem of Edward the First or Second's time, preserved in the British Museum, and intended to be one day given to the public. The two pieces will be found to afford a curious proof how poetry is preserved for a succession of ages by mere tradition; for though the imagery or description is nearly the same, the words are altogether different. Nor, had the "Canterbury Tales" of Chaucer been preserved to the present time in the same manner, would there have remained one single word which had fallen from the pen of that venerable bard; they would have been as completely, though not quite so elegantly, modernised as they are by Dryden and Pope; and yet it is pretended that the poems of Ossian have been preserved immaculate for more than a thousand years!

II. The pastoral simplicity, plaintive wildness, and animating hilarity of the Scotish music have long attracted universal attention: and the admiration of strangers, though it may not equal, is sufficient to justify the enthusiastic attachment of the natives. Wherever the taste has not been vitiated by the more artificial harmony of the Italian or German composer—in short, wherever there is nature or feeling—these "singularly sweet and pathetic melodies" (as they have been justly termed) cannot possibly fail to charm the imagination, and to interest the heart.

By whom, or under what circumstances, the original or most ancient Scotish tunes were invented or composed, it is now perhaps impossible to ascertain. The previous step, however, to an inquiry of this nature will be to determine which of the airs now extant are to be considered as the original or most ancient. A very ingenious writer, in an express "Dissertation on the Scotish Music," has tried to fix the era of the most ancient

Scotish melodies, and to trace the history of the Scotish music down to modern times—an attempt in which, as he has been guided rather by fancy and hypothesis than by argument or evidence, it is almost unnecessary to say that he has not succeeded. It is, however, but justice to add, that the subject is much indebted to a disquisition which evinces a considerable degree of ingenuity and a refined musical taste. "From their artless simplicity," he observes, "it is evident that the Scotish melodies are derived from very remote antiquity," while their "simplicity and wildness denote them to be the production of a pastoral age and country, and prior to the use of any musical instrument beyond that of a very limited scale of a few natural notes, and prior to the knowledge of any rules of artificial music. The most ancient," continues he, "of the Scotish songs still preserved, are extremely simple, and void of all art. They consist of one measure only, and have no second part, as the later or more modern airs have.* They must, therefore, have been composed for a very simple instrument, such as the shepherd's reed or pipe, of few notes, and of the plain diatonic scale, without using the semitones, or sharps and flats.† The distinguishing strain,"

---

* "Some old tunes," he observes, "have a second part, but it is only a repetition of the first on the higher octave, and probably of more modern date than the tunes themselves."

† "The only rule I could follow," he says, "was to select a few of the most undoubted ancient melodies, such as may be supposed to be the production of the simplest instrument of the most limited scale, as the shepherd's reed, and thence to trace them gradually downward to more varied, artful, and regular modulations, the compositions of more polished manners and times, and suitable to

he adds, " of our old melodies is plaintive and melancholy; and what makes them soothing and affecting to a great degree, is the constant use of the concordant tones, the third and fifth of the scale, often ending upon the fifth, and some of them on the sixth, of the scale. By this artless standard," he says, " some of our Scottish melodies may be traced—such as ' Gil Morrice,' ' There cam a Ghost to Marg'et's Door,' ' O Laddie, I man loo' thee,' ' Hap me wi' thy Pettycoat'—I mean," adds he, " the old sets of these airs, as the last air, which I take to be one of our oldest songs, is so modernised as scarce to have a trace of its ancient simplicity. The simple original air is still sung by nurses in the country as a lullaby to still their babes to sleep." The two last of these melodies, of which Mr Tytler observes, the artless simplicity of both words and music bears testimony of their originality and antiquity, are here inserted as proofs of the doctrine he has advanced, from copies obligingly communicated by himself :—

---

instruments of a more extended scale." A very little reflection, however, may serve to convince us that this rule is altogether fallacious, and can by no means determine the age of any melody whatever. Tunes may be, and probably are, composed to "the shepherd's reed " at this day; and the bagpipe, it must be remembered, has only nine notes. After all, what is meant by the " shepherd's *reed ?*" Is it the common flute? or stock and horn?

With respect to the melodies selected by Mr Tytler in support of his hypothesis, their antiquity is so very far from being "undoubted," that it seems altogether imaginary and chimerical. We by no means deny that the Scots either had or have ancient tunes or songs, we only (to adopt the words of Bishop Stillingfleet) " desire to be better acquainted with them."

F

DIALOGUE.

She.

O lad - ie, I man loo thee. O lass - ie, loo na

me. O lad - ie, I man loo thee. O lass - ie, loo na

me: For the lass - ie wi' the yel - low cot - tie has

stoun a - wa the heart frae me. O, &c.*

O hap me wi' thy pet - ty - coat, my ain kind thing, O

hap me wi' thy pet - ty - coat, my ain kind thing. The

wind blaws loud, my claith - ing's thin: O rise and let me in; And

hap me wi' thy pet - ty - coat, my ain kind thing.

* In the collection of old inedited Scotish ballads, mentioned in
a preceding page, are preserved the original melodies to which they
were sung by the lady from whose mouth they were taken down.
These, however, appear to have little resemblance to the characteristic genius of the Scotish music.

To return, however, to the origin of the Scotish music, which, waiving for the present the antiquity of particular tunes, we shall only consider in regard to the style of composition. Some, among whom is a very able writer, contend that "the honour of inventing the Scots music must be given to 'Ireland,' the ancient Scotia, from whence," he says, "the present Scotia derived her name, her extraction, her language, her poetry."* This con-

* Dr Campbell's "Philosophical Survey of the South of Ireland," p. 455, 1777.—That this music, or any one single Scotish air, was invented or composed by the unfortunate Rizzio, is only noticed here as an absurd fable; which, having no support, merits no refutation: and yet, it is very remarkable, almost every writer who has had occasion to touch upon the subject, appears particularly anxious to get rid of him; allowing, at the same time, that "perhaps he might have moulded some of the Scotch airs into a more regular form;" or that "he may have been one of the first, perhaps, who made a collection of these songs, or he may have played them with more delicate touches than the Scotch musicians of that time; or perhaps corrected the extravagance of certain passages;" suppositions for which there is just as little foundation as for the point in issue. "It is not probable," says Dr Gregory, "that a stranger . . . . should enter so perfectly into the taste of the national music, as to compose airs, which the nicest judges cannot distinguish from those which are certainly known to be of much greater antiquity than Rizzio's:" [which be they?] adding, that "the tradition on this subject is very vague, and there is no shadow of authority to ascribe any one particular tune to Rizzio."—*Comparative View*, &c., p. 1541. The learned writer's information seems to have been as inaccurate, as his ideas, or expressions at least, are confused; which might lead one to imagine that some show of management and dexterity was necessary even in combating a shadow. It may be worth inquiring, however, whether this formidable tradition have not been invented for the purpose of confutation; whether, in short, some one of those literary heroes have not actually made the giant he intended to demolish. Another equally groundless idea, that the Scotish music is indebted for its origin to the old church service, will be elsewhere

jecture is, indeed, by no means improbable ; but still it
is believed that there exists a sensible difference between
the native strains of Hibernia and the peculiar melodies
of the Lowland Scots, and that as well in the mournful
as in the festive strain.*   Giraldus Cambrensis, indeed,
who wrote before the year 1200, after praising the instrumental music of the Irish as beyond anything he had
been accustomed to, expressly says, that Scotland, by
reason of intercourse and affinity, and through scientific
emulation, endeavoured to imitate Ireland in musical

noticed.   It is to be regretted that one cannot trace these ridiculous
opinions back to their fountain-head.   Thompson, it is true, in the
index to "Orpheus Caledonius," positively asserts "that the songs
marked thus (*) were composed by David Rizzio.   These are, "The
Lass of Patie's Mill," "Bessie Bell," "The Bush aboon Traquair,"
"The Bonny Boatman," "An Thou were my Ain Thing," "Auld
Rob Morris," and "Down the Burn, Davie ;" but the assertion is a
proof at once of his ignorance and absurdity.

* Compare, for instance, the justly celebrated Irish airs of "Ellen
Aroon" and "Larry Grogan," with the no less famous Scotish
one of "Tweedside" and "The Bob of Dumblane ;" though it is
probable many other tunes might be contrasted with much greater
propriety and effect.   If, however, the "Birks of Endermay" be
originally an Irish tune, (a fact at the same time which requires
proof,) it will be difficult to controvert the point any further.   See
Walker's "Historical Memoirs of the Irish Bards," p. 128.   Dr
Beattie says expressly, that "the native melody of the Highlands
and Western Isles is as different from that of the southern parts of
the kingdom, as the Irish or Erse language is different from the
English or Scotch.   Of the Highland music," he adds, "the wildest
irregularity appears in its composition ; the expression is warlike
and melancholy, and approaches even to the terrible ;" while several
of the old Scotch songs "are sweetly and powerfully expressive of
love and tenderness, and other emotions suited to the tranquility of
a pastoral life ;" and he accounts for this difference in a very able
and ingenious manner.—*Essay on Poetry and Music.*

notes, and that, in the opinion of many at that day, she
not only equalled her mistress, but also in musical knowledge far excelled and surpassed her.* There is likewise
a passage in Martin's "Description of the Western
Islands," which has the appearance of a still stronger
authority in favour of Dr Campbell's position ; for there
can be no question as to the affinity of Irish and Highland music ; and perhaps it is of the latter we are to
understand the compliment cited from Giraldus, if indeed
the Lowland manners had begun to prevail in his time.
This author, (Martin,) speaking of the native inhabitants
of Skye, whom he describes as having a great genius for
music, says, "There are several of 'em who invent tunes
very taking in the south of Scotland and elsewhere ;"
adding, that " some musitians have endeavoured to pass
for first inventers of them by changing their name ; but
this has been impracticable, for whatever language gives
the modern name, the tune still continues to speak its
true original ; and of this," says he, "I have been shew'd
several instances," which, however, it is to be wished he
had condescended to particularise, as the late publication of Highland airs affords no support, it is believed,
to that hypothesis. After all, admitting the Irish origin
of the Scotish music, it cannot be reasonably doubted
that many, if not most, or even all of the most celebrated
and popular Scotish melodies, now extant, as distinguished from the Highland airs, have actually been
composed by natives of the Lowlands, speaking and
thinking in the English language ; by shepherds tending

---

* "Topographia Hiberniæ," Camden's "Anglica, Normannica,"
&c., p. 739, 1603.

their flocks, or by maids milking their ewes; by persons, in short, altogether uncultivated, or, if one may be allowed the expression, uncorrupted by art, and influenced only by the dictates of pure and simple nature.* The tunes now preserved must therefore have been noted by accident, numbers having doubtless perished, and perhaps daily perishing, of equal, or possibly greater, merit—

> " Full many a gem of purest ray serene
> The dark unfathom'd caves of ocean bear :
> Full many a flower is born to blush unseen,
> And waste its sweetness on the desert air." †

---

* The tune of " Weary fa' you, Duncan Gray," is said to have been the composition of a carman in Glasgow. — *Johnson's Scots Musical Museum*, vol. ii. (Index.)

† It was no small gratification to find this opinion as to the origin of Scotish music already enforced by so ingenious and elegant a writer as Dr Beattie, who believes " that it took its rise among men who were real shepherds, and who actually felt the sentiments and affections whereof it is so very expressive." Nature and indolence, no doubt, will occasionally produce similar effects in very distant and different countries. A late traveller found the quick tunes of the Moors in Barbary beautiful and simple, and partaking, in some degree, of the characteristic melody of the Scotish airs.— *Lempriere's Tour to Morocco*, p. 317, 1791. Nay, even in China, a country which has been civilised for ages, Dr Lind, an excellent judge of the subject, and philosophically curious in everything that relates to it, after residing there several years, assured Dr Burney that all the melodies he had heard, bore a strong resemblance to the old Scots tunes. " A very celebrated and learned physician," if one may venture to believe the editor of " Select Scotish Ballads," " who was born and passed his early years in the south of Scotland," informed him, that it was " his opinion that the best of the ancient Scotish airs were really composed by shepherds. In his remembrance there was, in almost every village of that district, a chief shepherd, who had acquired celebrity by composing better songs than others of the same profession ; and he thinks, that though the

This premised, it shall be the object of the present essay to collect such evidence as can be procured to illustrate the antiquity of the tunes in question.

As we have seen, the Scots had songs in the fourteenth century, so, no doubt, had they tunes or music to them ; but of what nature, and how far, if at all, resembling their now celebrated melodies, or if, indeed, anything more than the plain church chant, is at present almost beyond the reach of conjecture.

The tune of " Hey tutti taiti," to which there is a song, with those words in its burthen, beginning " Landlady, Count the Lawin," is said by tradition to have been King Robert Bruce's march at the battle of Bannockburn, in 1314.* It does not, however, seem at all probable that the Scots had any martial music in the time of this monarch, it being the custom at that period for every man in the host to bear a little horn, with the blowing of which, as we are told by Froissart, they would make such a horrible noise, as if all the devils of hell had been among them. It is not, therefore, likely that these unpolished warriors would be curious

---

best airs are in general known, yet the words to at least one-half have never been published."—*History of Music*, i. 38. A volume of these genuine inedited pastoral songs would be a very great curiosity.

Dr Burney, in the first volume of his " History of Music," p. 38, says, " The melody of Scotland will be hereafter proved of a much higher antiquity than has been generally imagined ;" but one looks in vain for the performance of this promise in the sequel of that elaborate work.

* Johnson's "Scots Musical Museum," vol. ii. (Index)—

" O Tite, tute Tati, *tibi tanta, tyranne tulisti*,"

in a line of Father Ennius.

> " to move
> In perfect phalanx to the Dorian mood
> Of flutes and soft recorders."

These horns, indeed, are the only music ever mentioned by Barbour,* to whom any particular march would have been too important a circumstance to be passed over in silence; so that it must remain a moot point whether Bruce's army were cheered by the sound of even a solitary bagpipe.

The battle of Harlaw, fought in 1411, gave name to a famous bagpipe tune, which preserved its celebrity till the middle of the last century :—

> " Interea ante alios dux piperlaius heros,
> Precedens, magnam que gerens cum burdine pipam,
> Incipit *Harlaii* cunctis sonare *battellum.*" †

King James I., who has been already mentioned as an excellent poet and song writer, was also an accomplished musician, and vocal as well as instrumental performer.‡ He is even celebrated (as is thought) by Tassoni, the well-known author of that original mock-heroic " La Secchia Rapita," in his book " De Diversi Pensieri," as having not only composed many sacred pieces of vocal

---

* " For we to morne her, all the day,
  Sall mak as mery as we may :
  And mak us boune agayn the nycht :
  And than ger mak our fyrs lycht :
  And blow our hornys, and mak far,
  As all the warld our awne war."
  —*The Bruce*, vol. iii. p. 148.

† Polemo-middinia. See before, p. 41.

‡ " Fordun," l. 16, cc. 28, 29. " He was weil lernit [in England]," says the translator of Boethius, " to synge and dance, and . . . . was richt crafty in playing baith of lute and harp, and sindry othir instrumentis of musik." According to Mr Tytler, he accompanied his own songs with the lute and harp; but this inference is not warranted by any ancient author.

music, but also of himself invented a new kind of music, plaintive and melancholy, different from all other, in which he had been imitated by Carlo Gesualdo, Prince of Venosa, who had improved music with new and admirable inventions.* This passage is regarded, by the ingenious writer so often quoted, as "perfectly characteristic of the pathetic strains of the old Scottish songs, and an illustrious testimony of their excellency." Since, however, no Scotish music, either of the composition or of the age of this monarch has been yet produced,† the

* Tassoni, it is observable, does not distinguish his royal musician from the five other princes of the same name who succeeded him : his words are merely, "*Noi possiamo connumerar tra nostri Jacopo re di Scozia,*" &c.,—that is, we may reckon among our modern composers James King of Scotland. Now, James I. had been dead for near a couple of centuries before Tassoni's book was written, (about 1610,) and was, consequently, at that period more of an ancient than a modern. Lord Kaimes, indeed, observes, that "the king mentioned must be James I. of Scotland," as he is the only one of their kings "who seems to have had any remarkable taste in the fine arts; an opinion," he adds, "in which all seem to be now agreed;" that "the music," however, "can be no other than the songs [he has] mentioned above," * is a different matter.—See *Sketches of the History of Man,* i. 166, 167.

† Mr Tytler, who thinks it scarce to be doubted that many of King James's compositions are still remaining, and make a part of the finest old Scotish melodies, though passing undistinguished, in all probability, under other names, and being adapted to modern words, says, that "of his age (some of them very probably of his composition) may be reckoned the following simple, plaintive, and ancient melodies :—"Jockie and Sandie," "Waly, Waly up the Bank," "Ay Waking, O !" "Be Constant ay," "Will ye go to the Ewe-bughts, Marrion," "Gil Morrice," "There cam a Ghost to

* "We have in Scotland a multitude of songs tender and pathetic, expressive of love in all its varieties of hope, fear, success, despondence, and despair. The style of the music is wild and irregular," &c.

above testimony, illustrious as it may be, is by no means
conclusive that this species of modulation was invented
by or even known to King James I. It is very remarkable, at the same time, that neither Mr Tytler, Lord
Kaimes, nor any other Scotish writer, who has brought
forward this celebrated passage, to prove that the native
music of Scotland was imitated, near two hundred years
ago, by an Italian prince, has thought it at all necessary
to produce or make any sort of inquiry after the imita-

Marg'et's Door," "O Laddie, I man loo' thee," "Hap me wi'
thy Pettycoat," he conjectures, from their artless simplicity, to
belong to an age prior to James I.   There is, in fact, no bound to
conjecture ; and it would be just as easy, and possibly just as true,
to fancy that all the old Scotish songs and tunes now extant, were
sung and played every day before Fingall, as he sat in his great
chair after dinner, "drinking the blude red wine," or promoting
the circulation of the social mull.   "How romantic," exclaims this
ingenious writer, "the melody of the old love ballad of 'Hero and
Leander!'   What a melancholy love story is told in the old song
of 'Jockie and Sandie!'"   They, however, who look for romantic
melody in the air, at least, of "Hero and Leander," will be probably
disappointed ; and the melancholy love story of "Jockie and Sandie"
seems calculated to excite laughter rather than tears; being in fact
a modern English imitation of an imaginary Scotish original, either
by, or very much, at least, in the style of Tom D'Urfey.   The first
line is best known, as people seldom read any more of it—

　　"Twa bonny lads were Sandie and Jockie."

Mr Tytler's zeal, indeed, has, on this occasion, betrayed him into a
little inconsistency.   To ascribe many or even any of the Scotish
popular airs to such a scientific musician as King James I., is utterly
incompatible with the original to which he has already allotted
them, and with the standard by which he contends their antiquity is
to be ascertained.   Besides, if some of these tunes existed before the
age of this monarch, he could not possibly be the inventor of that
peculiar style of music, and, consequently, Tassoni's compliment
must pass for nothing.

tions themselves. Now, it unluckily happens that the
works of this same prince of Venosa (who died in 1614)
have been repeatedly printed, and are by no means
difficult to procure. They consist of six sets of madrigals for five voices, and one for six. The ingenious Dr
Burney, who examined them with great attention, was
utterly unable to discover the least similitude or imitation of Caledonian airs in any one of them; which, so
far from Scotish melodies, seem, from his account, to
contain no melodies at all, and even to have as little
merit as possible in point of harmony. The doctor un-
derstands Tassoni's words to imply, " that these princely
dilettanti were equally cultivators and inventors of music;" adding, that if he meant otherwise, (to which one
may superadd even if he meant that,) his remarks must
have been hazarded either from conjecture or report.*
That the national music, therefore, was either invented
or improved by, or any way indebted to, King James I.,
there is every reason to disbelieve : unless by national
we are to understand cathedral music, to which he cer-

---

* "History of Music," iii. 218. If James VI., to whom a late
writer, less remarkable, indeed, for the justice than for the singu-
larity of his opinions, will have the above passage of Tassoni to
refer, and who was certainly a writer of madrigals, had actually
composed the music to them, there would remain little doubt of the
fact. It is, however, possible that some of these identical madrigals, set to music by one does not know whom, might have fallen
into the hands of Carlo Gesualdo, who, supposing the whole to pro-
ceed from the same royal genius, had immediately set himself to
imitate some peculiarities in the composition, which, if one may
judge by the character given of his own efforts, were altogether
unworthy of imitation.

tainly appears to have paid great attention.* He introduced the organ into churches, together with a new
method of singing, and gave great encouragement to
those skilled in it; and that he might, as Tassoni asserts,
compose " sacred pieces of vocal music," and even, like
our own Henry VIII., a canon in the unison, is sufficiently
credible; but will by no means prove that he was a cul-
tivator or even admirer of what we now mean by Scotish
music; between which and the compositions (whatever
they were) of King James I. there was probably the same
difference that must ever exist between pure nature and
mere art.†

Country dances appear, from this prince's own testimony, to have been a no less favourite amusement in his
time than they are at present. In his poem of " Peblis
to the Play," " The Schamon's Dance" is spoken of as a
well-known tune. ‡

King James IV. has the reputation of a composer.
In Johnson's " Scots Musical Museum" is a tune entitled " Here's a Health to my True Love," which is mentioned upon report as the performance of this gallant
monarch. One would be glad, however, of some better,

---

* See " Boethii Scotorum Historia," fo. 362.

† An absurd idea, said to prevail in Scotland, that the anthems
and services of the old church were sung to what are since become
popular melodies, will be noticed in another place.

‡ The word schamons cannot be explained. In the fragment of
a very old Scotish song, it is said, of a kind of fairy or genius,

" His legs were scarce a schathmont's length."

It has been very ridiculously interpreted showman's. See the Glossary to the present collection.

or at least earlier authority, as Scotish traditions are to be received with great caution.

The tune of " Flowden Hill," or " The Flowers of the Forest," is one of the most beautiful Scotish melodies now extant, and, if of the age supposed, must be considered as the most ancient. The " Souters of Selkirk," which has been already noticed, and is likewise a very fine air, if (as some say) it were actually composed upon the same occasion, must be left to dispute the precedency.*

The music of the " Gaberlunzie Man" is thought to be coeval with the words, if not by the same hand ; which is probably the case also with " The Beggar's Meal Pokes," and " Where Helen Lies." These three airs may therefore be esteemed the next in point of antiquity to those already mentioned.† The old ballad of " Johnie Armstrang" is accompanied, in a late musical publication, by a good melody, but of what age it is not perhaps easy to ascertain.

The long extract already given from Wedderburn's " Complainte of Scotlande," concluded with the shepherds beginning to dance in a ring, " euyrie ald scheiphyrd ' leading' his vyfe be the hand, and euyrie zong scheipird ' leading' hyr quhome he luffit best. There was viij scheiphyrdis," the author tells us, " and ilk ane of them hed ane syndry instrament to play to the laif." Having

---

* See before, p. 31.

† It may be here remarked, as somewhat singular, that tradition, which ascribes tunes, with whatever justice, to James IV. and James V., whose musical talents are unnoticed by any historical writer, should attribute nothing of the kind to James I., who is celebrated by several authors as another Apollo.

described these instruments, "kyng Amphion," he says, "that playit sa sueit on his harpe quhen he kepit his scheip, nor zit Apollo the god of sapiens, that kepit king Admetus scheip vitht his sueit menstralye, none of thir twa playit mayr cureouslye nor did thir viij schephyrdis befor rehersit; nor zit al the scheiphirdis that Virgil makkis 'mention' in his Bucolikis, thai culd nocht be comparit to thir foirsaid scheiphyrdis; nor Orpheus, that playit so sueit quhen he socht his vyf in hel, his play-ing prefferit nocht thir foirsaid scheiphirdis; nor zit the scheiphyrd Pan, that playit to the goddis on his bag-pype; nor Mercurius, that playit on ane sey reid, none of them could preffer thir foirsaid scheiphirdis. I beheld never ane mair dilectabil recreatione : for fyrst thai began vitht tua bekkis and vitht a kysse. . . . . It vas ane celest recreation to behald ther lycht lopene, galmoud-ing, stendling, bakuart & forduart, dansand base dansis, pauuans, galzardis, turdions, braulis, and branglis, buffons, vitht mony vthir lycht dancis, the quhilk ar ouer prolixt to be rehersit. Zit nochthles i sal rehers sa mony as my ingyne can put in 'memorie.' In the fyrst, thai dancit 'Al cristin mennis dance,' 'The northt of Scot-land,' 'Huntis vp,' * 'The commout entray,' 'Lang plat

---

* "Courage to give was mightily then blown
　'Saint Johnston's Huntsup,' since most famous known
　By all musicians, when they sweetly sing
　With heavenly voice and well concorded string."
　　　　　　　　　　　　　　—*Muses Threnedie.*

Again, in a poem "On May," by Alexander Scott, ("Ever Green," ii. 186 :)—

　　　" In May gois gallants bryng in symmer,
　　　And trymmly ocupy their tymmer
　　　　With 'hunt up' every morning plaid."

ful of gariau,' ' Robene Hude,' ' Thom of Lyn,' ' Freris
al,' ' Ennyrnes,' ' The loch of Slene,' ' The gosseps
dance,' ' Leuis grene,' ' Makky,' ' The speyde,' ' The
flail,' ' The lammes vynde,' ' Soutra,' ' Cum kyttil me
naykyt vantounly,' ' Schayke leg,' ' Fut befor gossep,'
' Rank at the rute,' ' Baglap and al,' ' Ihonne Ermi-
strangis dance,' ' The alman haye,' ' The bace of Vor-
agon,' ' Dangeir,' ' The beye,' ' The dede dance,' ' The
dance of Kilrynne,' ' The vod and the val,' ' Schaik a
trot.' Then quhen this dansing vas dune, tha departit
and past to cal their scheip cottis," &c. It is equally
singular and unfortunate, that not one of the dance-
tunes here named should be known to exist at this
moment.

"It is a received tradition in Scotland," says Dr
Percy, " that at the time of the Reformation, ridiculous
and obscene songs were composed, to be sung by the
rabble, to the tunes of the most favourite hymns in the
Latin service. ' Green Sleeves and Pudding Pies' (de-
signed to ridicule the Popish clergy) is said to be one
of those metamorphosed hymns : ' Maggy Lauder' was
another : ' John Anderson my Jo' was a third. The
original music of all these burlesque sonnets," continues
he, " was very fine." * This tradition is also mentioned

---

* The adaptation of solemn church music to these ludicrous
pieces, will account for the following fact. From the records of the
General Assembly in Scotland, called "The Book of the Universal
Kirk," p. 90, 7th July 1568, it appears that Thomas Bassendyne,
printer in Edinburgh, printed "a psalme buik, in the end whereof
was found printit ane baudy sang, called ' Welcome Fortunes.' "—
Reliques, &c., vol. ii. p. 122. One ought not, however, to have the
worse opinion of any poetical composition merely from the circum:-

by Mr Tytler, who gives it thus,—" That in ridicule of
the cathedral service, several of their hymns were, by
the wits among the reformed, burlesqued, and sung
as profane ballads.   Of this," he says, " there is
some remaining evidence.   The well-known tunes of
' John, come Kiss me now,' ' Kind Robin Lo'es me,'
and ' John Anderson my Jo,'* are said to be of that

stance of its being stigmatised with an opprobrious epithet by " the
universal kirk."

* " This tune was a piece of sacred music in the Roman Catholic
times of our country.   John Anderson is said by tradition to have
been town-piper in Kelso."—*Johnson's Scots Musical Museum*, vol.
iii. (Index.)   This identical song is preserved by Dr Percy.

WOMAN.

John Anderson my jo, cum in as ze gae bye,
And ze sall get a sheip's heid weel baken in a pye ;
Weel baken in a pye, and the haggis in a pat :
John Anderson my jo, cum in, and ze's get that.

MAN.

And how do ze, Cummer ? and how hae ze threven ?
And how mony bairns hae ze?   Wom. Cummer, I hae seven.
Man. Are they to zour awin gude man?   Wom. Na, Cummer, na
For five of them were gotten quhan he was awa.

The " seven bairns" are, with great probability, thought to allude
to the seven sacraments; five of which, it is observed, were the
spurious offspring of Mother Church : as the first stanza is supposed
to contain a satyrical allusion to the luxury of the Popish clergy,
which, however, is not so evident.   In Dr Percy's first edition the
second stanza ran thus :—

MAN.

And how doe ze, Cummer? and how do ze thrive?
And how mony bairns hae ze?   Wom. Cummer, I hae five.
Man. Are they all to zour ain gude man?   Wom. Na, Cummer, na ;
For three of tham were gotten quhan Willie was awa.

This, therefore, seems to have been the original ballad, of which the
satire was transferred, by the easy change of two or three words,
from common life to holy church.   It is, however, either way, a
great curiosity.

number."[*]   The evidence supposed to be here alluded
to, seems to prove a very different fact; which is, that
several common tunes were· pressed into the service of
the Puritans, in order either to satirise the Popish
clergy, or to promote their peculiar fanaticism, as has
been already mentioned.   No vestige of any Scotish
melody ever was or ever will be found in the old Scotish
Church service, which did not (for one of their service-
books is preserved) and could not possibly differ from
that of other Catholic countries, and must therefore have
consisted entirely of chant and counter point.   We may,
therefore, safely conclude that the Scotish song owes
nothing to the church music of the cathedrals and
abbeys before the Reformation; and that nothing can
be more opposite than such harmonic compositions to
the genius of song, which consists in the simple melody
of one single part.[†]   The tradition has probably no

---

[*] Tytler, p. 230. These hymns, unfortunately, were in Latin,
which, it is humbly presumed, "the wits among the reformed" un·
derstood somewhat too imperfectly to be able to burlesque them.
This part of the tradition is more absurd, if possible, than the other.

[†] Tytler, pp. 229, 230. As truth, not system, is the object of
this inquiry, the following communication, from a very ingenious
and much esteemed musical friend, appeared too interesting to be
suppressed:—"When I was in Italy, it struck me very forcibly that
the plain chants, which are sung by the friars or priests, bore a great
resemblance to some of the oldest of the Scotish melodies. If a
number of bass voices were to sing the air of 'Barbara Allan' in the
ecclesiastical manner, the likeness would appear so great[*] to a person who is not accustomed to hear the former frequently, that he
would imagine the one to be a slight variation from the other. That
accident might be the cause of original invention, the underwritten

---

[*] "Much more so than ' John, come kiss me now,' which, as the Scots say,
was originally a church chant."

other foundation than the ridiculous travestie, made by these pious reformers, of certain "prophaine sangs, for avoyding," as their cant is, "of sinne and harlotrie," and substituting a sort of blasphemous buffoonery in their place. "If," says Mr Tytler, "the other tunes, preserved of the old church music, were in the same style of 'John, come kiss me now,' our fine old melodies, I think, could borrow nothing from them." This, however, is not so clear; as "John, come kiss me now," is certainly a very fine tune.

It is uncertain whether the air to which "Rob's Jock" is sung or chanted be coeval with the original words, which appear to have been popular in 1568. Could the point be ascertained, it is probably one of the oldest Scotish song-tunes now extant.

The music, as well as the words, of "The Bonny Earl of Murray," may be reasonably supposed contemporary with the event of his murder. "Tak your Auld Cloak about ye," and "Waly, waly up the bank," have been already mentioned as productions of the sixteenth century; the air of each is a fine, and probably genuine, specimen of ancient Scotish melody.

The next piece of Scotish music of which one is able

---

will prove. About twelve years ago, on trying my pianoforte, after tuning, by putting my fingers casually (with some degree of musical rhythmus) upon the short keys, avoiding the long ones, it surprised me much to hear an agreeable Scots melody. This is so curious and so certain, that those who are totally ignorant of music, may amuse themselves by playing the same measure and motion of any well-known tune upon the short keys only, which in modern instruments are made of ebony, to distinguish them from the long ones, which are generally made of ivory."

to fix the date is " General Leslie's March," 1644. That
the Aberdeen collection, printed in 1666, contains many
songs of a much earlier period, we have a right to infer
from the preservation of "O Lusty May with Flora Queen,"
which is known to have been popular in 1549. The air
of that song, and of the others inserted from the same
book in the present volume, will be sufficient to show
that the characteristic melody of Scotland is under very
little obligation to its compiler.   At the end of the same
publication are three singular compositions for as many
voices, which are conjectured to have been sung by
peasants in the Christmas holidays before the Reformation ; the music is a church chant."*

* See extracts from one of these pieces before, p. 48. They are
all very rude, and their antiquity is collected from the following
lines :—

> " All sones of Adam, rise up with me,
> Go praise the blessed Trinitie, &c.
> Then spake the archangel Gabriel, said, Ave, Mary mild,
> The Lord of lords is with thee, now shall you go with child :
> *Ecce ancilla domini.*

> " Then said the virgin, as thou hast said, so mat it be,
> Welcom be heaven's king.
> There comes a ship far sailing then,
> Saint Michel was the stieres-man ;
> Saint Iohn sate in the horn :
> Our Lord harped, our lady sang,
> And all the bells of heaven they rang,
> On Christ's sonday at morn," &c.

In the " Pleugh song," all " the hyndis" are named, and all things
belonging to the plough enumerated ; the ploughman's cries to his
oxen are given, and the like; but it will not bear transcribing.   In
the third edition of this work, printed at Aberdeen in 1682, (which
Mr Pinkerton " wishes very much to see,") this " pleugh song," and
the pieces which follow it, are omitted, and "severall of the choisest
Italian-songs, and new English-ayres," inserted in their stead.   The
tenor part, certainly, and the bass part, probably, appeared at the
same time.

No direct evidence, it is believed, can be produced of the existence of any Scotish tune now known prior to the year 1660, exclusive of such as are already mentioned; nor is any one, even of those, to be found noted, either in print or manuscript, before that period.

Ramsay, in his "Tea-Table Miscellany," published, as before observed, in 1724, remarks of the Scotish tunes, that though they "have not lengthened variety of music, yet they have an agreeable gaiety and natural sweetness that make them acceptable wherever they are known, not only among ourselves, but in other countries. They are, for the most part," he says, "so cheerful, that, on hearing them well played or sung, we find it a difficulty to keep ourselves from dancing;" and, "what further adds to the esteem we have for them is their antiquity, and their being universally known." This passage is the rather noticed, as being the earliest testimony hitherto met with of the excellence and antiquity of Scotish music.* From the two first volumes of Ramsay's collec-

* The following tunes, to which there are new words in the "Tea-Table Miscellany," appear from that circumstance to have been popular at the time of its publication:—"Polwarth on the Green," "Woe's my Heart that we should sunder," "Carle and the King come," "Auld Lang Syne," "Hallow Ev'n," "I wish my Love were in a Mire," "The Fourteenth of October," "The Broom of Cowden Knows," "The Bonniest Lass in a' the Warld," "The Boatman," "The Kirk wad let me be," "Saw ye my Peggy," "Blink over the Burn, Sweet Betty," "The Bonny Grey-ey'd Morning," "Logan Water," "For our Lang Biding here," "My Apron deary," "I fixed my Fancy on her," "I loo'd a Bonny Lady," "Gilder Roy," "The Yellow-hair'd Laddie," "When she came ben she bobed," "John Anderson my Jo," "Come kiss with me, come clap with me," "Rothes's Lament; or Pinky House," "Tibby Fowler in the Glen," "Where shall our Good Man ly," "Allan Water; or, My Love

tion, " Mr Thomson," he tells us, who was "allowed by all to be a good singer and teacher of Scots songs, culled his 'Orpheus Caledonius,' the music for both the voice and flute, and the words of the songs, finely engraven in a folio book for the use of persons of the highest quality in Britain, and dedicated to the late queen." * Notwithstanding this compliment, Mr Thomson does not appear to have been a man of either taste or genius; his selection is by no means judicious, and the few pieces not immediately taken from Ramsay of little merit.† A very

Annie's very bonnie," "Where Helen lies," "Gallowshiels," "Ranting, Roaring Willie," "Sae merry as we have been," "Steer her up and had her gawn," "Bessy's Haggies," "Lochaber no more," "Valiant Jocky," "When absent, &c.," "Gillikranky," "The Happy Clown," "Jenny beguil'd the Webster," "Busk ye, busk ye, my Bonny Bride," "We'll a' to Kelso go," "Montrose's Lines," "Widow, are ye wawkin," "The Glancing of her Apron," "Auld Sir Simon the King," (English,) "Through the Wood, Laddie," "A Rock and a Wee Pickle Tow," "The Highland Laddie," "Bessy Bell," "The Bonny Lass of Branksome," "The Wawking of the Faulds," "O Dear Mother, what shall I do," "How can I be sad on my Wedding Day," "Cauld Cale in Aberdeen," "Mucking of Geordy's Byer," "Leith Wynd," "O'er Bogie," "O'er the Hills and far away."

* "Orpheus Caledonius; or, A Collection of the Best Scotish Songs, set to musick by W. Thomson, London, engraved and printed by the author, at his house in Leicester-fields," fo. no date. [1725?] Dedicated "To Her Highness the Princess of Wales," (afterwards Queen.) The second edition was published, with an additional volume, in 8vo, 1733.

† That Thomson either did not understand, or did not attend to what he published, is apparent from the following blunder, which is repeated in his second edition :—

> " My apron is made of *a Lyncum* twine
> Well set about wi' pearling *Syne*."

A Lyncum should be *the Lyncum*, (*i. e.* Lincoln,) and *Syne* should be *fine*. Though a certain prolific writer, whose confidence is more

small collection of tunes for the " Tea-Table Miscellany," either before or soon after the appearance of Thomson's work, was published by Ramsay himself.

The insurrections of 1715 and 1745 seem to have inspired all the pipers in Scotland, having given rise to almost as many tunes as would fill a volume. Of these some have correspondent words, while those of others bear so little proportion to the merit of the melody as to be either lost or neglected. A few of the rest will be found in the present collection, one of which is the subject of an interesting anecdote related in Mr Arnot's " History of Edinburgh."*

remarkable than his veracity, has been pleased to assert that " Lincum licht is a common Glasgow phrase for very light," and that "no particular cloth was ever made at Lincoln," every one knows the latter part of the assertion to be false, which seems a sufficient reason for disbelieving the former part of it to be true.

* " After the rebellion, 1745, the divided spectators frequently displayed in the theatre a spirit of political dissension. Upon the anniversary of the battle of Culloden, 1749, this animosity rose to a height which threatened consequences of a serious nature. Certain military gentlemen who were in the playhouse called out to the band to play ' Culloden,' [a tune composed in order to keep up the remembrance of the bloody defeat of an unfortunate party.] This was regarded by the audience as ungenerously and insolently upbraiding the country with her misfortunes. Resenting it accorddingly, they ordered the band to play, ' You 're welcome, " Charlie " Stuart.' The musicians complying, instantly a number of officers attacked the orchestra, with drawn swords, and leaped upon the stage. Among them was the son of a chieftain, who had drawn the Pretender on to his rash attempt, by offering to join him with his clan, and who, upon the prince's landing, raised his clan, it is true; but, instead of fulfilling his engagement, joined the royal army. This young gentleman leaping upon the stage, to display the zealousness of his loyalty, slipped his foot, and fell flat upon the stage. The spectators being tickled with the circumstance, an immense

About the year 1750, Mr Oswald, a musicseller in London, published a large collection of Scotish tunes under the title of " The Caledonian Pocket Companion," a work in which he must have exerted prodigious industry. The number of airs in these twelve volumes (which are, however, thin enough to bind up together in one) is not less than between five and six hundred, and includes many very ancient, very excellent, and very curious pieces, nowhere else to be found, nor ever before published. The following favourite airs—" Alloa House," " The Banks of Forth," " Roslin Castle," " The Braes of Ballendine," and several others, were composed by Oswald himself, of whom Mr Tytler observes, that his genius in composition, joined to his taste in the performance of Scotish music, was natural and pathetic.

A smaller collection was edited about the same period by M'Gibbon, who, as well as Oswald, indulges himself a little too much in affected variations. Selected songs and melodies have been since published by Bremner,

---

peal of laughter burst through the house, which exasperated the indignation of the officers. Meantime, fiddle-sticks being unable to cope with polished steel, the musicians fled; but the military were not long able to remain masters of the field. They were assailed from the galleries with apples, snuff-boxes, broken forms, in short, with everything missile that could be laid hold of. The officers at once consulted their safety, and went in quest of revenge, by quitting the stage, in order to attack the galleries, which they stormed sword in hand. The inhabitants of these upper regions defended themselves from the fury of the soldiers, by barricading their doors. The Highland chairmen, learning the nature of the quarrel, with their poles attacked the officers in the rear, who, being neither able to advance nor retreat, were obliged to surrender at discretion, leaving the chairmen masters of the field."—P. 374.

Sutherland & Corri, Napier, and Johnson—in the last of which, entitled " The Scots Musical Museum," (in four volumes,) are many curious pieces, not, it is believed, to be elsewhere met with.

The object of the preceding inquiry has been to discover facts, not to indulge conjecture. Those songs and tunes, therefore, of which intrinsic evidence alone may be supposed to ascertain the age, are left to the genius and judgment of the connoisseur; such, for instance, as " Hero and Leander," " Lady Ann Bothwell's Lament,"* " Muirland Willie," " Ay waking, oh !" " The Lowlands of Holland," " Ewebughts Marion," " The Blythsome Bridale," " My Jo Janet," " Auld Rob Morris," " Rare Willie drown'd in Yarrow," " Katherine Ogie,"† " Maggy

* Mr Tytler classes these two ballads together in his second epoch, that is, in the reigns of James IV., James V., and Queen Mary; but then he does the same by " Leader Haughs and Yarrow," which has all the appearance of a song not older than the present century. All his epochs, indeed, are perfectly fanciful and un-founded. The editor of " Select Scotish Ballads" pretends, that in a quarto manuscript in his possession, " containing a collection of poems, by different hands, from the reign of Queen Elizabeth to the middle of the last century, when it was apparently written, there are two balowes, as they are there styled, the first, ' The balow, Allan,' the second, ' Palmer's balow;' this last," he says, " is that commonly called ' Lady Bothwell's Lament,' and the three first stanzas in this [his own] edition are taken from it, as is the last from ' Allan's balow.' They are injudiciously mingled," he adds, " in Ramsay's edition, and several stanzas of his own added." Part of this is certainly false, and the rest of it probably so. Though some words, and even lines, of Ramsay's copy are different from that in the " Scots poems," 1706, the number of stanzas is the same in both.

† Was " sung by Mr Abell, at his concert in Stationers' Hall," about 1680.

Lauder,"* "Sweet William's Ghost," "Johny Faa," &c. It is, however, to be hoped that the future researches of the antiquaries of Scotland will be so diligent and successful, as to leave no doubts either on this or any other branch of their national antiquities.

The era of Scotish music and Scotish song is now passed.† The pastoral simplicity and natural genius of former ages no longer exist ; a total change of manners has taken place in all parts of the country, and servile imitation usurped the place of original invention. All, therefore, which now remains to be wished is, that in-

* Dr Percy, in his " Essay on the Ancient English Minstrels," p. xxxvii., observes, that " in the old song of ' Maggy Lawder,' a piper is asked, by way of distinction, ' come ze frae the Border?' " Now, without meaning to dispute the antiquity of the song, though it cannot surely be very great, it may be fairly assumed that the learned essayist never met with a copy, either printed or manuscript, so antiquated as to have the *z* substituted for the *y*. Any modern ballad, though but written yesterday, might, by this curious Chattertonian manœuvre, (in the use or abuse of which Dr P. is supposed not to have been very sparing,) pass for one of two or three hundred years old. Maggie's question, at the same time, is not, " Come ye frae," but

" Live you upo' the Border?"

which, it is probable, many of his profession might do, for the con· veniency of attending fairs and public meetings in both kingdoms. That this tune was popular at the Reformation, or about the middle of the sixteenth century, is utterly incredible.

† Those who presume, at present, to direct the public taste in regard to Scotish music, seem totally insensible of the merit of the original songs, thinking it necessary to engage the prolific (if not prostituted) muse of Peter Pindar, to supply them with new words by contract. They have only afterward to hire some Italian fiddler, of equal eminence, to furnish them with tunes, and the business will be complete. The practice, however ingenious, is by no means unprecedented. See before, p. 56.

dustry should exert itself to retrieve and illustrate the relics of departed genius.

III. A few words should, and but a few can, be added concerning the ancient musical instruments of the Scots, of which, perhaps, they have at no period possessed any great variety. These instruments, in the time of Sylvester Giraldus, were the harp, or cythara, tympanum, and chorus. The tympanum resembled the tabor, tambour de Basque, or tambourin, and the chorus was a sort of double trumpet, of which the form is preserved in Luscinius's " Musurgia," printed at Strasburg in 1536. The continuator of Fordun mentions James I. as a masterly performer on the tympanum and chorus, as well as on the psaltery and organ, the tibia and lyra, the tuba and fistula—words which one cannot pretend to translate— adding that he touched the harp (cythara) like another Orpheus ;* and the translator of Boethius expressly mentions, that "he was richt crafty in playing baith of the lute and harp, and sindry othir instrumentis of musik." Notwithstanding these authorities, it seems highly probable that the harp was chiefly confined to the Highlanders, whom, along with their Irish brethren, Major notices as excellent performers upon that instrument, although it is now totally unknown in the Highlands,†

* l. 16, c. 28.

† " The last of these strolling harpers," says Mr Tytler, " was Rory or Roderick Dall, [*i. e.* blind Roderick,] who, about fifty years ago, was well known and much caressed by the Highland gentry, whose houses he frequented. His chief residence was about Blair in Athole, and Dunkeld. He was esteemed a good composer, and a fine performer on the harp, to which he sang in a pathetic man-

as there appears no other evidence of its having ever been in use among the Lowland Scots.

The bagpipe may be regarded as the national instrument, being a universal favourite with the people, to whom it has afforded a grateful harmony for many centuries, being introduced by the royal bard among the disorderly festivities of " Peblis to the Play"—

> " With that Will Swane come sweitand out,
>   Ane meikle millar man,
> Giff I sall dance, haue doune, lat se
> Blaw up the bagpyp than. *

The young folks were also summoned out in the morning by the same exhilarating sound—

> " The bag-pyp blew, and they out threw
> Quite from the townis vntald."

Thus also, in the epilogue to Sir David Lindsay's " Satyre of the Thrie Estaits," (written in 1539,†) the speaker says—

---

ner. Many of his songs," he adds, " are preserved in that country." —*Dissertation*, &c. See also M'Donald's essay, " Of the Influence of Poetry and Music upon the Highlanders," prefixed to his " Collection of Highland Airs." Another blind harper, named Tuskne, is mentioned in one of Dr Pennecuik's poems, at the end of his " Description of Tweeddale," Edin. 1715.

* From a subsequent stanza we learn that the piper would have been very well contented with

> " Thre happenis for half ane day :"

though, moderate as his demands were, they appear not to have been complied with; the company, which was numerous, being probably unable to raise a sum equal to about half an English farthing; for which the musician very charitably bids " the meikill deuill gang with" them.

† This date is ascertained beyond the possibility of a doubt, by a curious original letter from Sir William Eure to some nobleman of

> " Menstrell, blaw up ane brawl of France,
>   Let se quha hobbils best." *

When or how this instrument first found its way into this
country is almost beyond the reach of conjecture.   The
tradition of the Hebrides gives its introduction to the
Danes or Norwegians, who were long possessed of these

---

the English court, dated Berwick, 26th January [1539.]   There had
been a Border meeting at Coldstream on the 21st of that month, at
which Sir William was informed, by Master Bellendyn, one of the
Scotish commissioners, that "by the kinges pleasour, he being prevey
therunto, they 'had' hade ane enterluyde played in the feaste of
the epiphane of our lorde last paste, before the king and quene at
Lighqwoe, and the hoole counsaile spirituall and temporall."   He
likewise transmits a copy of " the nootes of the interluyde," which,
says he, " I haue obteigned from a Scottesman of our sorte, being
present at the playing of the saide enterluyde."   These notes contain a particular description of the piece in question, which evidently
appears to have been Lindsay's " Satyre of the thrie estaits."   This
important communication is preserved in a MS. of the royal library
in the Museum, (7 C XVI.) and clearly proves that James V. was
better inclined to a reformation of religion than he appeared to be
to Sir Ralph Sadler.   So that it is by no means an argument of
Mackenzie's folly to tell us that Lindsay's works were first printed
at Edinburgh in 1540: "as if," exclaims Mr Pinkerton, "works
against the Papists could, in 1540, be printed at Edinburgh!"   With
submission to this dashing genius, one may reasonably presume, that
if such works could be publicly represented at Lithgow in 1539,
they might safely be printed at Edinburgh in 1540.   The expressions, inconsistent with the above date, in the Hyndford MS., must
of course have been introduced after the original representation.

 * It is clear, from this passage, that French dance tunes were in
fashion at that period, as indeed we learn from another place—

> " Now hay for ioy and mirth I dance,
>   Tak thair ane gamond of France."

What, if any, resemblance exists between the old French and modern Scotish music, must be left to the researches of the musical
antiquary.

islands,* which is sufficiently probable. There can be
no question, indeed, either as to the antiquity or univer-
sality of this instrument; we find it to have been well
known to the Greeks and Romans, and it is at this day
common in Italy and Germany. It must be observed,
however, that the pipe at present used in the low country, or south of Scotland, is essentially different from the
old Highland pipe, which is uniformly blown with the
breath, whereas the former, like the Irish pipe, is filled
by means of a bellows.†

* M'Donald's essay.

† The merit of originality, it must be confessed, appears due to
the Highland pipe; the other being probably of almost recent introduction. Habbie Simson, who flourished in the latter part, as it
is supposed, of the seventeenth century, was undoubtedly a Lowland piper; but the idea given in the title to the excellent elegy on
his death, viz.,

> " Who on his drone bore bonny flags;
> He made his cheeks as red as crimson,
> And babbed when he blew the bags,"

incontestably proves that his instrument was the Highland pipe.
The song of " Maggie Lauder " is still more modern. It celebrates
the performance of a famous piper, who, though he lived upon the
Border, did not make use of a bellows; since, we find, he played
his part so well, that his cheeks were "like the crimson." Para-
doxical, therefore, as it may appear, the Lowland pipes were probably introduced out of England, in which country this species of
bagpipe is a very ancient, as it was once a very common instrument. " As melancholy as the drone of a Lincolnshire bagpipe,"
is one of Falstaff's similes in the first part of Shakespeare's " King
Henry the Fourth;" * and "a Yorkshire bagpiper" occurs in
another proverbial saying. Performers, in short, on this instrument, which Chaucer has put into the hands of his pilgrim miller,
(though it must be confessed that, as represented in one of the rude
cuts in Caxton's edition, he blows the pipe with his mouth,) were

* See also Fuller's " Worthies," p. 152.

In "The Houlate," an allegorical poem by one Holland, written about 1450, a number of musical instruments is enumerated, most, if not all, of which were probably then in use. The stanza alluded to is as follows :—

> " All thus our ladye thai lofe, wi h lyking and lift,
> Menstralis and musicians, mo than I mene may,
> The psaltry, the citholis, the soft atharift,
> The 'croude' and the monycordis, the gythornis gay,
> The rote, and the recordour, the ribus, the rift,
> The trump, and the taburn, the tympane but tray ;
> The li t pype, and the lute, the cithill and fift,
> The dulsate, and the dulsacordis, the schalin of affray ;
> The amyable organis usit full oft ;
> Clarions loud knellis,
> Portatibis, and bellis,
> Cymbaellonis in the cellis,
> That soundis so ' soft.'" *

Of the eight shepherds mentioned in Wedderburn's "Complainte," "the fyrst hed ane drone bagpipe, the

formerly of sufficient consequence to be upon the household establishment of the English monarchs, and are still retained by the Duke of Northumberland. See "Ancient Songs," p. xiii., (1790 ;) "Reliques of Ancient English Poetry," vol. i. p. xxxvi. For much curious and interesting information relative to the history and performance on the bagpipe, see Pennant's "Tour in Scotland" in part I., p. 374, (1772 ;) Macdonald's essay, (already cited ;) Walker's "Historical Memoirs of the Irish Bards," p. 75; Encyclopædia Britannica," article BAGPIPE.

* Scotish Poems, iii. 179, (1792.) Of these instruments some have been already, or will be hereafter explained, some require no explanation, and some are incapable of it. See "Ancient Songs," p. xli., &c., (1790.) The lilt-pype is, probably, the bag-pipe. Cymbaellonis are cymbals. It is remarkable that no mention is here made of the harp, which may seem to confirm the idea of its not being of general use in the Lowlands, even in the time of James I.

nyxt hed ane pipe made of ane bleddir and of ane reid, the third playit on ane trump,* the feyrd on ane corne

* Ane trump, is a Jew's trump, an instrument of great antiquity, for which see Pennant's "Tour in Scotland" in 1769, 4to, p. 215. This was the favourite music of the Scotish witches in the time of that sapient monarch James VI. "Agnes Tompson 'being' brought before the king's maiestie and his councell . . . . confessed that vpon the night of All hollon euen last shee was accompanied as well with the persons aforesaide, as also with a great many other witches, to the number of two hundreth ; and that they all together went to sea, each one in a riddle or ciue,* and went in the same very substantially, with flaggons of wine, making merrie and drinking by the way in the same riddles or ciues, to the kirke of North Barrick in Lowthian ; & that after they had landed, tooke handes on the lande and daunced this reill or short daunce, singing all with one voice,

"Commer goe ye befor, commer goe ye,
Gif ye will not goe before, commer let me."

At which time shee confessed that this Geilles Duncan [a servant girl] did goe before them playing this reill or daunce vpon a small trumpe, called a Jewes trump, vntill they entred into the kerk of North Barrick. These confessions made the king in a wonderfull admiration, and sent for the saide Geillis Duncane, who vpon the like trump did play the saide daunce before the kinges maiestie ; who in respect of the strangenes of these matters, tooke great delight to be present at their examination."—*Newes from Scotland*, &c., 4to, b. l., (1591). The devil, however, being doubtless a much better musician than Geillis Duncane, was wont to entertain his fair votaries with the sound of the harp or bagpipe. A witch, being demanded if she ever had any pleasure in the devil's company, "Never much," said she ; "but one night going to a dancing upon Pentland hills, he went before us, in the likeness of a rough tanny dog, playing on a pair of pipes : the spring he played was, 'The silly bit chiken, gar cast it a pickle, and it will grow meikle.'" This good lady appears to have paid pretty dearly for her pleasure, had it been more exquisite ; she and her husband, according to the en-

* To this passage Shakespeare was indebted for the idea of his witch sailing in a sieve. See "Macbeth," act 1, scene 3.

pipe,* the fyft playit on ane pipe maid of ane gait horne,
the sext playit on ane recordar, [a small flute or flageolet,]

lightened piety of the age, being both burned alive. Some of the
Swedish witches confessed that the devil used to "play upon a harp
before them ;" but this, it seems, was only when he was amorously
disposed. He did not, however, always condescend to perform,
having, like other great men, a piper retained in his service ; and
only amusing himself with the composition of love songs, and their
attendant airs. "A reverend minister," says our author, "told me,
that one, who was the devil's piper, a wizard, confessed to him,
that at a ball of dancing the foul spirit taught him a baudy song, to
sing and play, as it were this night ; and ere two days passed, all
the lads and lasses of the town were lilting it through the street." It
were abomination to rehearse it.—See "Satan's Invisible World
Discovered." It is a pity, however, that the air, at least, was not
preserved; as we know, from Corelli's account of his most celebrated sonata, that his infernal majesty is an excellent composer ;
and the accompaniment of a Presbyterian hymn would have proved
a sufficient antidote against its most diabolical effects. The trump
or Jew's harp, according to both Martin and Macdonald, is the only
musical instrument of the St Kildians. It disposes them, however,
to dance mightily, and they have a number of reels.

* A corn pipe is a horn pipe, *pipeau de corne.* The instrument
is mentioned is Spenser's "Shepherd's Calendar :"—

> "Before them yode a lusty taberere,
> That to the many on a horne pype played,
> Whereto they dauncen eche one with his mayd,
> To see these folkes make suche jouisance,
> Made my heart after the pype to daunce."

This, it has been conjectured, is the instrument alluded to by Ramsay in his "Gentle Shepherd :"—

> "When I begin to tune my stock and horn,
> With a' her face she shaws a cauldrife scorn," &c.

Which he explains in a note to be "a reed or whistle, with a horn
fixed to it by the smaller end." The figure of this instrument may
be seen under the ingenious Mr Allan's head of Ramsay prefixed to
his elegant edition of the "Gentle Shepherd," as well as in the first
of those beautiful and characteristic designs with which it is orna-

the seuint plait on ane fiddill, and the last plait on ane quhissil."

We learn from a curious passage in Brantome, (already quoted,) that the good people of Edinburgh used to accompany their psalms with wretched fiddles and small rebecs, of which he says there was no want in the country. The vocal and instrumental performances, or rather poetry and music, of these godly reformers seem to have been admirably suited to each other.

The violin has been encroaching for some time on the province and popularity of the bagpipe, and will one day most probably, as it has very nearly done in England, silence it entirely—an event which some ignorant or conceited pipers, by endeavouring to strain the instrument to exertions it is incapable of, seem desirous to accelerate.[*] Great praise, however, is due to the Highland Society for the encouragement it gives to performers of merit by an annual prize.

mented. See also the vignette (by the same excellent artist) on the title-page of the present volume.

Richard Brathwaite, however, ("Strappado for the Deuill," 1615,) has a poem addressed "To the queen of harvest, &c., much honoured by the reed, corn pipe, and whistle ;" and it must be remembered that the shepherd boys of Chaucer's time had

—— " many a floite and litlyng horne,
And pipes made of grené corne ;"

and also that, in the "Midsummer Night's Dream," Titania reproaches the fairy king for having

—— " in the shape of Corin sate all day,
Playing on pipes of corn, and versing love
To amorous Phillida."

* See " Encyclopædia Britannica," article BAGPIPE, and M'Donald's Essay, p. 14.

In the hope that this investigation, which, dry, tedious, and imperfect as it is, will perhaps be occasionally found to throw a glimmering light upon a subject hitherto obscure, may hereafter provoke the exertions of some person qualified, in point of erudition, information, musical knowledge, taste, and language, to do it justice, these pages are concluded with satisfaction.

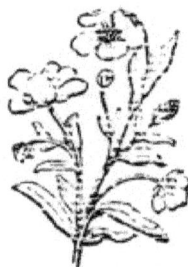

SCOTISH SONGS.

" Then you, whose symphony of souls proclaim
  Your kin to heaven, add to your country's fame ;
  And shew that musick may have as good fate
  In Albion's glens, as Umbria's green retreat ;
  And with Correlli's soft Italian song
  Mix ' Cowden Knowes,' and ' Winter Nights are Long.'"

RAMSAY.

CLASS THE FIRST.

SONG I.

BY WILLIAM HAMILTON OF BANGOUR, ESQ.

Set by COUNT ST GERMAIN.

[O] wouldst thou know her sa - cred charms,

Who this des - tined heart a - larms, Who this

des - tined heart a - larms, What kind of nymph the

heavens de - cree, What kind of nymph the hea - - - -

- - - - - - - - - - vens

de - cree, The maid that's made for love and me.

Who pants to hear the sigh sincere,
Who melts to see the tender tear,
From each ungentle passion free;
Such the maid that's made for me.

Who joys whene'er she sees me glad,
Who sorrows when she sees me sad,
For peace and me can pomp resign;
Such the heart that's made for mine.

Whose soul with gen'rous friendship glows,
Who feels the blessing she bestows,
Gentle to all, but kind to me;
Such be mine, if such there be.

Whose genuine thoughts, devoid of art,
Are all the natives of her heart,
A simple train, from falsehood free;
Such the maid that's made for me.

Avaunt, ye light coquets, retire,
Whom glittering fops around admire,
Unmov'd your tinsel charms I see,
More genuine beauties are for me.

Should Love, fantastic as he is,
Raise up some rival to my bliss,
And should she change, but can that be?
No other maid is made for me.

SONG II.

BY ALLAN RAMSAY.*

TUNE—"The waukin' o' the fauld."

My Peg - gy is a young thing, Just en-ter'd in her teens, Fair

as the day, and sweet as May, Fair as the day, and al - ways gay. My

Peg - gy is a young thing, And I'm no ve - ry auld, Yet

weel I like to meet her at The wauk - in' o' the fauld.

My Peg - gy speaks sae sweet - ly, When-e'er we meet a - lane, I

wish nae mair to lay my care, I wish nae mair o' a' that's rare. My

Peg - gy speaks sae sweet - ly, To a' the lave I'm cauld; But

she gars a' my spi - rits glow, At wauk - in' o' the fauld.

* In the "Gentle Shepherd."

My Peggy smiles sae kindly,
    Whene'er I whisper love,
That I look down on a' the toun,
That I look down upon a croun.
    My Peggy smiles sae kindly,
        It makes me blythe and bauld,
And naething gi'es me sic delight,
        As waukin' o' the fauld.

    My Peggy sings sae saftly,
        When on my pipe I play ;
By a' the rest, it is confest,
By a' the rest, that she sings best.
    My Peggy sings sae saftly,
        And in her sangs are tauld
Wi' innocence the wale of sense,
        At waukin' o' the fauld.

SONG III.

TWEEDSIDE.*

BY ROBERT CRAWFORD.

What beau-ties does Flo - ra dis - close! How sweet are her
smiles up - on Tweed! Yet Ma - ry's still sweet - er than

* Several of the ideas in this beautiful pastoral are closely imitated from Solomon's song.

those, Both na - ture and fan - cy ex - ceed. Nor

dai - sy, nor sweet blush - ing rose, Not all the gay

flowers of the field, Not Tweed glid - ing gent - ly thro'

those. Such beau - ty and plea - sure does yield.

The warblers are heard in the grove,
   The linnet, the lark, and the thrush,
The blackbird, and sweet cooing dove,
   With musick enchant ev'ry bush.
Come, let us go forth to the mead,
   Let us see how the primroses spring ;
We 'll lodge in some village on Tweed,
   And love while the feather'd folks sing.

How does my love pass the long day ?
   Does Mary not tend a few sheep ?
Do they never carelessly stray,
   While happily she lies asleep ?
Tweed's murmurs should lull her to rest ;
   Kind nature indulging my bliss,
To relieve the soft pains of my breast,
   I 'd steal an ambrosial kiss.

'Tis she does the virgins excel,
  No beauty with her may compare;
Love's graces around her do dwell,
  She's fairest where thousands are fair.
Say, charmer, where do thy flocks stray!
  Oh! tell me at noon where they feed;
Shall I seek them on sweet winding Tay,
  Or the pleasanter banks of the Tweed!

SONG IV.

TO MRS A. H. ON SEEING HER AT A CONCERT.

BY ROBERT CRAWFORD.

TUNE—"The Bonniest Lass in a' the Warld."

Look where my dear Ha - mil - la smiles, Ha - mil - la!

hea - ven - ly charm-er; See how with all their

arts and wiles The Loves and Grac - es arm her. A

blush dwells glow - ing on her cheeks, Fair seats of

youth - ful plea-sures, There Love in smil - ing

lan - guage speaks, There spreads his ros - y trea - sures.

O fairest maid, I own thy pow'r,
 I gaze, I sigh, and languish,
Yet ever, ever will adore,
 And triumph in my anguish.
But ease, O charmer, ease my care,
 And let my torments move thee ;
As thou art fairest of the fair,
 So I the dearest love thee.

———◆———

SONG V.

AN THOU WERE MY AIN THING.

An thou were my ain thing, I would lo'e thee,

I would lo'e thee; An thou were my ain thing, How

dear - ly would I lo'e thee! Of race di - vine thou

needs must be, Since no-thing earth-ly e-quals thee; For hea-ven's

DA CAPO.

sake, oh! fa-vour me, Who on-ly "live" to lo'e thee.

The gods one thing peculiar have,
To ruin none whom they can save;
O! for their sake, support a slave,
 Who only lives to lo'e thee.
   An thou were, &c.

To merit I no claim can make,
But that I love; and, for " thy " sake,
What man can name I 'll undertake,
 So dearly do I lo'e thee.
   An thou were, &c.

My passion, constant as the sun,
Flames stronger still, will ne'er have done,
Till Fates my thread of life have spun,
 Which breathing out I 'll lo'e thee,
   An thou were, &c.

SONG VI.

THE YELLOW-HAIR'D LADDIE.*

BY ALLAN RAMSAY.

In A-pril, when prim - ros - es paint the sweet
plain, And sum-mer ap-proach-ing re-joic-eth the
swain, The yel-low-hair'd lad-die would oft-en
times go, To wilds and deep glens, where the
haw - thorn trees grow. haw - thorn trees grow.

---

* THE AULD YELLOW-HAIR'D LADDIE.

The yellow-hair'd laddie sat down on yon brae,
Cries, Milk the ewes, lassie, let nane of them gae ;
And aye she milked, and aye she sang,
The yellow-hair'd laddie shall be my gudeman.
     And aye she milked, &c.

The weather is cauld, and my claithin' is thin ;
The ewes are new clipped, they winna bught in ;
They winna bught in, tho' I should dee :
O yellow-hair'd laddie, be kind to me.
     They winna bught in, &c.

There, under the shade of an old sacred thorn,
With freedom he sang his loves ev'ning and morn ;
He sang with so soft and enchanting a sound,
That sylvans and fairies unseen danced around.

The shepherd thus sang, Though young Maya be fair,
Her beauty is dash'd with a scornful, proud air ;
But Susie was handsome, and sweetly could sing,
Her breath like the breezes perfumed in the spring.

That Madie, in all the gay bloom of her youth,
Like the moon was unconstant, and never spoke truth ;
But Susie was faithful, good-humour'd, and free,
And fair as the goddess who sprang from the sea.

That mamma's fine daughter, with all her great dow'r,
Was awkwardly airy, and frequently sour ;
Then, sighing, he wished, would parents agree,
The witty sweet Susie his mistress might be.

The gudewife cries butt the house, Jenny, come ben,
The cheese is to mak, and the butter's to kirn ;
Tho' butter, and cheese, and a' should sour,
I 'll crack and kiss wi' my love ae hauf hour ;
It 's ae hauf hour, and we 'se e'en mak it three,
For the yellow-hair'd laddie my husband shall be.

SONG VII.

KATHARINE OGIE.

As walk-ing forth to view the plain, Up - on a

morn - ing ear - ly, While May's sweet scent did cheer my

brain, From flowers which grow so rare-ly, I chanced to

meet a pret - ty maid, She shin'd tho' it was

fo - gie: I ask'd her name, Sweet sir, she said,

My name is Kath - arine O - gie.

I stood a while, and did admire
To see a nymph so stately;
So brisk an air there did appear
In a country maid so neatly:
Such natural sweetness she display'd,
Like a lily in a bogie;
Diana's self was ne'er array'd
Like this same Katharine Ogie.

Thou flow'r of females, beauty's queen,
　　Who sees thee sure must prize thee;
Tho' thou art drest in robes but mean,
　　Yet these cannot disguise thee:
Thy handsome air, and graceful look,
　　Far excels any clownish rogie;
Thou 'rt match for laird, or lord, or duke,
　　My charming Katharine Ogie.

O were I but some shepherd swain,
　　To feed my flock beside thee,
At bughting time to leave the plain,
　　In milking to abide thee;
I 'd think myself a happier man,
　　With Kate, my club, and dogie,
Than he that hugs his thousands ten,
　　Had I but Katharine Ogie.

Then I 'd despise th' imperial throne,
　　And statesmen's dangerous stations;
I 'd be no king, I 'd wear no crown,
　　I 'd smile at conquering nations;
Might I caress and still possess
　　This lass, of whom I 'm vogie;
For these are toys, and still look less
　　Compar'd with Katharine Ogie.

But I fear the gods have not decree'd
　　For me so fine a creature,
Whose beauty rare makes her exceed
　　All other works of nature:

Clouds of despair surround my love,
    That are both dark and fogie;
Pity my case, ye powers above!
    Else I die for Katharine Ogie.

SONG VIII.

THE LASS O' PATIE'S MILL.

BY ALLAN RAMSAY.

The lass o' Pa-tie's mill, Sae bon-nie, blyth, and gay, In spite o' a' my skill, She stole my heart a-way. When ted-din' out the hay, Bare-head-ed on the green, Love 'midst her locks did play, And wan-ton'd in her een.

Her arms, white, round and smooth,
    Breasts rising in their dawn,
To age it would give youth,
    To press them with his hand.

I

Thro' all my spirits ran
    An ecstasy of bliss,
When I such sweetness fand
    Wrapt in a balmy kiss.

Without the help of art,
    Like flowers which grace the wild,
She did her sweets impart,
    Whene'er she spoke or smiled.
Her looks they were so mild,
    Free from affected pride ;
She me to love beguiled,
    I wish'd her for my bride.

Oh, had I all that wealth
    Hopetoun's high mountains* fill,
Insured long life and health,
    And pleasure at my will ;
I'd promise and fulfil,
    That none but bonnie she,
The lass o' Patie's mill,
    Should share the same wi' me.

---

* " Thirty-three miles south-west of Edinburgh, where the Right
Honourable the Earl of Hopetoun's mines of gold and lead are."—
Ramsay.

SONG IX.

ON CELIA PLAYING ON THE HARPSICHORD AND SINGING.

BY TOBIAS SMOLLETT, M.D.

When Sap-pho struck the qui-v'ring wire, The
throb-bing breast was all on fire: And when she
raised the vo-cal lay, The cap-tive soul was
charm'd a-way: And when she raised the vo-cal
lay, The cap-tive soul was charm'd a-way.

But had the nymph possess'd with these
Thy softer, chaster power to please;
Thy beauteous air of sprightly youth;
Thy native smiles of artless truth;

The worm of grief had never prey'd
On the forsaken, love-sick maid:
Nor had she mourn'd a hapless flame,
Nor dash'd on rocks her tender frame.

SONG X.

BY ALLAN RAMSAY.*

TUNE—" Winter was cauld, and my claithin' was thin." †

PEGGY.

WHEN first my dear laddie gaed to the green hill,
And I at ewe-milking first say'd my young skill,
To bear the milk-bowie nae pain was to me,
When I at the bughtin' forgather'd with thee.

PATIE.

When corn-riggs waved yellow, and blue heatherbells
Bloom'd bonnie on moorland and sweet rising fells,
Nae birns, briers, or breckans gied trouble to me,
If I found the berries right ripen'd for thee.

PEGGY.

When thou ran or wrestled, or putted the stane,
And cam' aff the victor, my heart was aye fain ;
Thy ilka sport manly gied pleasure to me,
For nane can putt, wrestle, or run swift as thee.

PATIE.

Our Jenny sings saftly the " Cowden Broom-Knowes,"
And Rosie lilts swiftly the " Milking the Ewes ;"
There's few " Jenny Nettles" like Nancy can sing,
At " Thro' the Wood, Laddie," Bess gars our lugs ring :

* In the "Gentle Shepherd."   † See note p. 125.

But when my dear Peggy sings, wi' better skill,
The " Boatman," " Tweedside," or the " Lass o' the
    Mill,"
It 's mony times sweeter and pleasin' to me ;
For tho' they sing nicely, they cannot like thee.

PEGGY.

How easy can lassies trow what they desire !
And praises sae kindly increases love's fire :
Gie me still this pleasure, my study shall be
To mak' myself better and sweeter for thee.

SONG XI.

ETTRICK BANKS.

On Et-trick banks, on a sum-mer's night, At gloam-in'
when the sheep drave hame, I met my lass-ie braw and
tight, Come wad-in', bare-foot, a' her lane : My
heart grew light, I ran, I flang My arms a-bout

her   li - ly   neck,   And   kiss'd and clapp'd her
there fu' lang,   My   words   they   were   na   mo - ny   feck.

I said, My lassie, will ye gang
    To the Highland hills, the Earse to learn?
I 'll gie thee baith a cow and ewe,
    When ye come to the Brig o' Earn.
At Leith auld meal comes in, ne'er fash,
    And herrings at the Broomielaw ;
Cheer up your heart, my bonnie lass,
    There 's gear to win ye never saw.

A' day when we hae wrought eneugh,
    ᐧ When winter frosts and snaws begin,
Soon as the sun gaes west the loch,
    At night when ye sit down to spin,
I 'll screw my pipes and play a spring ;
    And thus the weary night will end,
Till the tender kid and lamb time bring
    Our pleasant simmer back again.

Syne, when the trees are in their bloom,
    And gowans glint o'er ilka fiel',
I 'll meet my lass amang the broom,
    And lead you to my summer shiel' :

Then far frae a' their scornfu' din,
   That mak the kindly hearts their sport,
We 'll laugh and kiss, and dance and sing,
   And gar the langest day seem short.

———◆———

SONGS XII. AND XIII.

THE YOUNG LAIRD AND EDINBURGH KATIE.

BY ALLAN RAMSAY.

Now wat ye wha I met yes-treen, Com-in' down the
street, my jo? My mis-tress in her tar-tan screen, Fu'
bon-nie, braw, and sweet, my jo. My dear, quoth I, thanks
to the night, That ne-ver wish'd a lo-ver ill, Sin' ye're out
o' your mi-ther's sight, Let's tak a walk up to the hill.

O Katie, wilt thou gang wi' me,
   And leave the dinsome toun a while?
The blossom 's sproutin' frae the tree,
   And a' the simmer 's gaun to smile:

The mavis, nightingale, and lark,
   The bleatin' lambs, and whistlin' hynd,
In ilka dale, green shaw, and park,
   Will nourish health, and glad your mind.

Soon as the clear gudeman o' day
   Does bend his mornin' draught o' dew,
We'll gae to some burnside and play,
   And gather flowers to busk your brow :
We'll pou the daisies on the green,
   The lucken gowans frae the bog ;
Between hands now and then we'll lean,
   And sport upon the velvet fog.

There's up into a pleasant glen,
   A wee piece frae my father's tower,
A canny, saft, and flowery den,
   Which circlin' birks have form'd a bower :
Whene'er the sun grows high and warm,
   We'll to the caller shade remove ;
There will I lock thee in mine arm,
   And love and kiss, and kiss and love.

KATIE'S ANSWER.

BY ALLAN RAMSAY.

My mi-ther's aye glow-rin' o'er me, Tho' she did the same be-fore me: I can-na get leave To look to my love, Or else she'd be like to de-vour me. Right fain wad I tak your of-fer, Sweet sir, but I'll tyne my to-cher; Then, San-dy, ye'll fret, And wyte your poor Kate, When-e'er ye keek in your toom cof-fer.

For tho' my father has plenty
Of siller and plenishin' dainty,
   Yet he's unco sweir
    To twin wi' his gear;
And sae we had need to be tenty.

Tutor my parents wi' caution,
Be wylie in ilka motion ;
　　Brag weel o' ye'r land,
　　And there 's my leal hand,
Win them, I 'll be at your devotion.

SONG XIV.

BY JOSEPH MITCHELL.

TUNE—" Pinkie House."

By Pin - kie House oft let me walk, While, cir - cled in my arms, I hear my Nell - y sweet - ly talk, And gaze on all her charms. Oh, let me ev - er fond be - hold Those grac - es void of art! Those cheer - ful smiles that sweet - ly hold In will - ing chains my heart.

Oh come, my love ! and bring anew
  That gentle turn of mind ;
That gracefulness of air, in you
  By Nature's hand design'd.
What beauty, like the blushing rose,
  First lighted up this flame,
Which, like the sun, for ever glows
  Within my breast the same !

Ye light coquettes ! ye airy things !
  How vain is all your art !
How seldom it a lover brings !
  How rarely keeps a heart !
Oh, gather from my Nelly's charms,
  That sweet, that graceful ease ;
That blushing modesty that warms ;
  That native art to please !

Come, then, my love ! oh, come along !
  And feed me with thy charms ;
Come, fair inspirer of my song !
  Oh, fill my longing arms !
A flame like mine can never die,
  While charms so bright as thine,
So heav'nly fair, both please the eye,
  And fill the soul divine.

SONG XV.

TUNE—"The Banks of the Forth." *

A - wake, my love; with ge - nial ray The
sun, re - turn - ing, glads the day; A - wake, the
balm - y ze - phyr blows, The haw - thorn blooms, the
dai - sy glows, The trees re - gain their ver - dant
pride, The tur - tle woos his ten - der
bride, To love each war - bler tunes the song, And
Forth in dim - ples glides a - long.

* Composed by Mr Oswald.

Oh more than blooming daisies fair !
More fragrant than the vernal air !
More gentle than the turtle-dove,
Or streams that murmur through the grove !
Bethink thee, all is on the wing,
These pleasures wait on wasting spring ;
Then come, the transient bliss enjoy ;
Nor fear what fleets so fast will cloy.

———◆———

SONG XVI.

BY DAVID MALLET.

TUNE—" The Birks of Invermay."

The smil-ing morn, the breath-ing spring, In - vite the
tune - ful birds to sing: And while they war - ble from each
spray, Love melts the u - ni - ver - sal lay. Let
us, A - man - da, time - ly wise, Like them, im-

prove the hour that flies, And, in soft rap - tures,

waste the day, A - mong the shades of In - ver - may.

For soon the winter of the year,
And age, life's winter, will appear ;
At this thy living bloom must fade,
As that will strip the verdant shade.
Our taste of pleasure then is o'er ;
The feather'd songsters love no more ;
And when they droop, and we decay,
Adieu the shades of Invermay !

———◆———

SONG XVII.

AN ADDRESS TO HIS MISTRESS.

BY WILLIAM FALCONER.

Set by Mr SHIELD.

The smil - ing plains, pro-fuse - ly gay, Are dress'd in all the

pride of May; The birds on ev' - ry spray a - bove To

rap - ture wake the vo - cal grove. But, ah, Mi - ran - da,

with - out thee, Nor spring nor sum - mer smiles on me: All

lone - ly in the se-cret shade, I mourn thy absence, charm-ing maid.

Oh soft as love ! as honour fair !
Serenely sweet as vernal air !
Come to my arms, for you alone
Can all my " anguish " past atone !

Oh come ! and to my bleeding heart
The sovereign balm of love impart ;
Thy presence lasting joy can bring,
And give the year eternal spring !

———◆———

SONG XVIII.

BY JAMES THOMSON.

Tune—" Logan Water."

For e - ver, For-tune, wilt thou prove An un - re-

lent - ing foe to love ; And when we meet a mu - tual

heart, Come in be - tween, and bid us part: Bid us sigh on from

day to day, And wish, and wish the soul a-way; Till

youth and ge - nial years are flown, And all the

life of life is gone?

But busy, busy still art thou,
To bind the loveless, joyless vow,
The heart from pleasure to delude,
And join the gentle to the rude.

For once, O Fortune, hear my prayer,
And I absolve thy future care ;
All other blessings I resign,
Make but the dear Amanda mine.

SONG XIX.

Tune—"Cumbernauld House."

From anx - ious zeal and fac - tious strife, And
all th'un - eas - y cares of life, From beau - ty
still to me - rit blind, And still to fools and
cox - combs kind; To where the woods, in bright - est green, Like
ris - ing the - a - tres are seen, Where gent - ly mur - m'ring
runs the rill, And draws fresh streams from ev' - ry hill.

Where Philomel, in mournful strains,
Like me, of hopeless love complains,
Retired I pass the livelong day,
And idly trifle life away:
My lyre to tender accents strung,
I tell each slight, each scorn and wrong,
Then reason to my aid I call,
Review past scenes, and scorn them all.

K

Superior thoughts my mind engage,
Allured by Newton's tempting page,
Through new-found worlds I wing my flight,
And trace the glorious source of light :
But should Clarinda there appear,
With all her charms of shape and air,
How frail my fix'd resolves would prove !
Again I 'd yield, again I 'd love !

———◆———

SONG XX.

BY WILLIAM HAMILTON OF BANGOUR.

Slow.   Set by Mr SHIELD.

Go, plain-tive sounds, and to the fair My se-cret wounds im-part: Tell all I hope, tell all I fear, Each mo - tion in my heart. But she methinks is list'ning now To some enchanting strain, The smile that triumphs o'er her brow, Seems not to heed my pain.

* The last verse to be sung a little quicker.

Yes, plaintive sounds, yet, yet delay,
  Howe'er my love repine,
Let that gay minute pass away,
  The next perhaps is thine.
Yes, plaintive sounds, no longer cross'd,
  Your griefs shall soon be o'er,
Her cheek, undimpled now, has lost
  The smile it lately wore.

Yes, plaintive sounds, she now is yours,
  'Tis now your time to move ;
Essay to soften all her powers,
  And be that softness love.
Cease, plaintive sounds, your task is done
  That anxious tender air
Proves o'er her heart the conquest won,
  I see you melting there.

Return, ye smiles, return again,
  Return each sprightly grace,
I yield up to your charming reign,
  All that enchanting face.
I take no outward show amiss,
  Rove where they will her eyes,
Still let her smiles each shepherd bless
  So she but hear my sighs.

SONG XXI.

BLINK OVER THE BURN, SWEET BETTY.

In sum-mer I mawed my mea-dow, In har-vest

I shure my corn, In win-ter I mar-ried a

wi-dow, I wish I was free the morn! Blink

o-ver the burn, sweet Bet-ty, Blink o-ver the

burn to me: Oh, it is a thou-sand

pi-ties But I was a wi-dow for thee.

SONG XXII.

LOW DOUN IN THE BROOM.

BY JAMES CARNEGIE.

Lively.

My dad-die is a can-ker'd carle, He'll nae twin wi' his
gear; My min-nie she's a scald-ing wife, Hauds a' the house
a-steer: But let them say, or let them do, It's
a' ane to me; For he's low doun, he's in the broom, That's
wait-in' on me: Wait-in' on me, my love, He's wait-in' on
me, For he's low doun, he's in the broom, That's wait-in' on me.

My auntie Kate sits at her wheel.
And sair she lightlies me;
But weel ken I it's a' envy,
For ne'er a jo has she.
But let them, &c.

My cousin Kate was sair beguiled
   Wi' Johnnie o' the glen ;
And aye sin syne she cries, Beware
   Of fause deluding men.
      But let them, &c.

Gleed Sandy he cam wast ae night,
   And spier'd when I saw Pate ;
And aye sin syne the neighbours round
   They jeer me air and late.
      But let them, &c.

SONG XXIII.

AYE WAKIN', OH.

Aye wak-in' oh, Wak-in' aye and wea-rie, Sleep I
can-na get, For think-in' o' my dea-rie. When I sleep
I dream, When I wake I'm ee-rie; Rest I can-na
Da Capo.
get, For think-in' o' my dear-ie.

SONG XXIV.

WILL YE GO TO FLANDERS, MY MALLY, O?

Slow.

Will ye go to Flan - ders, My Mal - ly, O?

Will ye go to Flan-ders, my bon - nie Mal - ly, O? There

we'll get wine and bran-dy, And sack and su - gar-can - dy.

Will ye go to Flan-ders, my Mal - ly, O?

Will ye go to Flanders, my Mally, O!
And see the chief commanders, my Mally, O!
    You'll see the bullets fly,
    And the soldiers how they die,
And the ladies loudly cry, my Mally, O.

SONG XXV.

EWE-BUGHTS, MARION.

Will ye go to the ewe-bughts, Ma - rion, And wear in the sheep wi' me? The sun shines sweet, my Ma - rion, But nae half sae sweet as thee. Oh Ma - ri - on's a bon - nie lass, And the blythe blink's in her e'e; And fain wad I mar - ry Mar - ri - on, Gin Ma - rion wad mar - ry me.

There's gowd in your garters, Marion,
    And silk on your white-hause bane;
Fu' fain wad I kiss my Marion,
    At e'en when I come hame.
There's braw lads in Earnslaw, Marion,
    Wha gape, and glower with their e'e,
At kirk when they see my Marion;
    But nane of them loves like me.

I 've nine milk ewes, my Marion,
    A cow and a brawny quey ;
I 'll gi'e them a' to my Marion,
    Just on her bridal day ;
And ye 'se get a green sey apron,
    And waistcoat o' London broun,
And wow but ye 'll be vap'rin',
    Whene'er ye gang to the toun.

I 'm young and stout, my Marion ;
    Nane dances like me on the green ;
And gin ye forsake me, Marion,
    I 'll e'en gae draw up wi' Jean ;
Sae put on your pearlins, Marion,
    And kyrtle o' cramasie ;
And soon as my chin has nae hair on,
    I shall come west, and see ye.

Will ye go to the ewe - bughts, Ma - rion, And
wear in the sheep wi' me? The sun shines sweet, my
Ma-rion, But nae half sae sweet as thee. The sun
shines sweet, my Ma-rion, But nae half sae sweet as thee.

SONG XXVI.

Tune—"To daunton me." *

Alas! when charming Sylvia's gone,
I sigh and think myself undone ;
But when the lovely nymph is here,
I 'm pleased, yet grieve ; and hope, yet fear,
Thoughtless of all but her I rove :
Ah! tell me, is not this call'd love ?

Ah me ! what power can move me so ?
I die with grief when she must go,
But I revive at her return ;
I smile, I freeze, I pant, I burn :
Transports so strong, so sweet, so new,
Say, can they be to friendship due ?

Ah no ! 'tis love, 'tis now too plain,
I feel, I feel the pleasing pain ;
For who e'er saw bright Sylvia's eyes,
But wish'd, and long'd, and was her prize ?
Gods, if the truest must be bless'd,
O let her be by me possess'd.

* See Song XXXIV., Class III.

SONG XXVII.

TO A LADY, ON HER TAKING SOMETHING ILL THAT MR H. HAD SAID.

BY WILLIAM HAMILTON OF BANGOUR.

TUNE—"Hallowe'en."

Why hangs that cloud upon thy brow, That beauteous
heav'n erewhile serene? Whence do these storms and
tempests blow? Or what this gust of passion mean?
And must then mankind lose that light, Which
in thine eyes was wont to shine, And lie obscured in
endless night, For each poor silly speech of mine?

Dear child, how could I wrong thy name?
Thy form so fair, and faultless stands,
That could ill tongues abuse thy fame,
Thy beauty would make large amends:

* Mrs S. H.—*Ramsay.*

Or if I durst profanely try
　　Thy beauty's powerful charms t' upbraid,
Thy virtue well might give the lie,
　　Nor call thy beauty to its aid.

For Venus every heart t' ensnare,
　　With all her charms has deck'd thy face,
And Pallas, with unusual care,
　　Bids wisdom heighten every grace.
Who can the double pain endure?
　　Or who must not resign the field
To thee, celestial maid, secure
　　With Cupid's bow and Pallas' shield?

If then to thee such power is given,
　　Let not a wretch in torment live,
But smile, and learn to copy Heaven,
　　Since we must sin ere it forgive.
Yet pitying Heaven not only does
　　Forgive th' offender and th' offence,
But even itself appeased bestows,
　　As the reward of penitence.

SONG XXVIII.

HAUD AWA' FRAE ME, DONALD.*

Oh come a - wa', come a - wa', Come a - wa' wi'
me, Jen - ny; Sic frowns I can - na bear frae
ane, Whase smiles ance ra - vish'd me, Jen - ny.
If you 'll be kind, you 'll ne - ver find That aught shall
al - ter me, Jen - ny; For you 're the mis - tress of
my mind, What - e'er you think of me, Jen - ny.

First when your sweets enslaved my heart,
    You seem'd to favour me, Jenny;
But now, alas! you act a part
    That speaks inconstancie, Jenny;

* A song to which this name and tune are supposed to have originally belonged is inserted in Part II.

Inconstancie is sic a vice,
 It 's not befitting thee, Jenny;
It suits not with your virtue nice,
 To carry sae to me, Jenny.

------◆------

HER ANSWER.

O HAUD awa', haud awa',
 Haud awa' frae me, Donald;
Your heart is made o'er large for ane,
 It is not meet for me, Donald:
Some fickle mistress you may find,
 Will jilt as fast as thee, Donald;
To ilka swain she will prove kind,
 And nae less kind to thee, Donald.

But I 've a heart that 's naething such,
 It 's fill'd with honestie, Donald;
I 'll ne'er love " many," I 'll love much,
 I hate all levitie, Donald.
Therefore nae mair with art pretend
 Your heart is chain'd to mine, Donald:
For words of falsehood " ill" defend
 A roving love like thine, Donald.

First when you courted, I must own,
 I frankly favour'd you, Donald;
Apparent worth and fair renown
 Made me believe you true, Donald:

Ilk virtue then seem'd to adorn
    The man esteem'd by me, Donald;
But now the mask 's faun off, I scorn
    To ware a thocht on thee, Donald.

And now, for ever, haud awa',
    Haud awa' frae me, Donald;
Gae seek a heart that 's like your ain,
    And come nae mair to me, Donald:
For I 'll reserve mysel' for ane,
    For ane that 's liker me, Donald;
If sic a ane I canna find,
    I 'll ne'er lo'e man, nor thee, Donald.

DONALD.

Then I 'm thy man, and fause report
    Has only tauld a lie, Jenny;
To try thy truth, and make us sport,
    The tale was raised by me, Jenny.

JENNY.

When this ye prove, and still can love,
    Then come awa' to me, Donald;
I 'm well content ne'er to repent
    That I have smiled on thee, Donald.

SONG XXIX.

I'LL NEVER LOVE THEE MORE.

BY JAMES THE GREAT MARQUIS OF MONTROSE.

My dear and on - ly love, I pray, "This lit - tle"
world of thee, Be go-vern'd by no o - ther sway But
pu - rest mon - arch - ie: For if con - fu - sion have a
part, Which vir - tu - ous souls ab - hor, "I'll call" a sy - nod
in my heart, "And" ne - ver love thee more.

As Alexander I will reign,
　　And I will reign alone,
My thoughts "did" evermore disdain,
　　A rival on my throne.
He either fears his fate too much,
　　Or his deserts are small,
"Who dares not put" it to the touch,
　　To "gain" or lose it all.

But I must rule and govern still,
    And always give the law ;
And have each " subject" at my will,
    And all to stand in awe :
But 'gainst my batteries if I find
    Thou " storm or vex me" sore,
As " if" thou set me " as" a blind,
    I 'll never love thee more.

Or in the empire of thy heart,
    Where I should solely be,
Another do pretend a part,
    And dare to vie with me ;
Or if committees thou erect,
    And " go " on such a score,
I 'll, " smiling, mock " at thy neglect,
    And never love thee more.

But if " no faithless action stain "
    Thy "love and constant" word,
I 'll make thee " famous" by my pen,
    And " glorious" by my sword.
I 'll serve thee in such noble ways,
    " As ne'er was known" before ;
I 'll crown and deck thy head with bays,
    And love thee " more and " more.

——◆——

SONG XXX.

SLIGHTED LOVE SAIR TO BIDE.*

Where art thou, Hope, that pro-mised me re - lief?

Come, hear my doom pro-noun-ced by dis - dain. Come,

trai - tor Hope, that all men doth mis-chief, Come here,

let see, and ease me of my pain. A-lace! sweet Hope,

where is thy scope? Or where shalt thou re-main? Why flees thou

me, to make me die? Wilt thou not come a - gain? Since Hope

is gone, and can-not me re-mead, In bon-dage thus I

must bide For-tune's fead, I must bide For - tune's fead.

* Written before 1666. The title was prefixed by Ramsay, who omitted the 1st, 3d, 4th, 6th, and 8th stanzas. The music has been in parts, but the cantus or tenor appears to have been the only one ever published. The antiquity of this song was the chief induce-ment to its insertion.

I had a heart, and now I heartless go :
I had a mind that dayly was opprest :
I had a friend that's now become my fo :
I had a will, yet I can get no rest.
    What have I now? nothing I trow,
    But spite where I had joy :
    What am I then? a heartless man :
    Should love me thus destroy?
I love and serve one whom I do regard,
Yet, for my love, disdain is my reward.

If promised faith, and secret love intend,
And choose but doubt, I thought I had done well.
If fixed eye and inward heart do bind
A man in love, as now my heart doth feel :
    What pain is love? or what may move
    A man for to despair?
    Nothing so great as hie despite
    Of his sweet lady fair :
Such is my chance, as now I must confess ;
I love a love, though she be merciless.

What pain can pierce a heart that I do want.
If love be pain that doth any subdue?
What pain can force a body to be faint?
If love be pain, how can I pain eschew?
    Since I am fast, knit to the mast,
    This torment to endure ;
    And have no might, by law nor right,
    My lady to procure :
What shall I say, since will gain-stands the law?
I have a will, yet will makes me stand aw.

Where shall I go to hide my weary face?
Where shall I find a place for my defence?
Where is my love, who is the meetest place
Of all the earth that is my confidence :
    She hath my heart, till I depart,
    Let her do what she list ;
    I cannot mend, but still depend,
    And dayly to insist
To purchase love, if love my love deserve ;
If not for love, let love my body sterve.

Come here, ye gods, and judge my cause aright :
Hear my complaint before ye me condemn :
Take you before my lady most of might :
Let not the wolf devore the silly lamb.
    If she may say, by night or day,
    That ever I did her wrong ;
    My mind shall be, with cruelty,
    To ly in prison strong :
Then shall ye save a sakeless man from pain ;
Try well my cause, and then remove disdain.

O lady fair, whom I do honour most,
Your name and fame within my breast I have :
Let not my love and labour thus be lost ;
But still in mind, I pray you to ingraff,
    That I am true, and shall not rue
    A word that I have said :
    I am your man, do what ye can,
    When all these playes are play'd.
Then save your ship unbroken on the sand,
Since man and goods are all at your command.

Then choose to keep or loss that you have done :
Your friendly friend doth make you this request :
Let not friends come us lovers two between,
Since late detests caused you me to detest.

    Keep hope in store, you to deplore,
    Conquer your friend indeed :
    Remember aye, will come the day,
    When friends a friend will need :·
You have a friend so friendly and so true,
Keep well your friend : I say no more.   Adieu.

———◆———

SONG XXXI.

THE VAIN ADVICE.*

BY MRS COCKBURN.

Slow.   Set by Mr SHIELD.

Ah! gaze not on those eyes! For - bear that soft in-
chant - ing voice to hear: Not looks of ba - si - lisks give
sur - er death, Not Sy - rens sing with more de-

* This song ought not to have been inserted, as the authoress,
though of Scotch parentage, was born in London.

struc-tive breath. Fly, if thy free - dom thou'dst main - tain ; A-

las! I feel th' ad - vice is vain: A heart, whose safe - ty

but in flight does lye, Is too far lost to have the pow'r

to fly, Is to far lost to have the pow'r to fly.

SONG XXXII.

BY THOMAS BLACKLOCK, D.D.

TUNE—"The Braes o' Ballendine."

Be - neath a green shade a love - ly young

swain One eve-ning re - clined to dis - co - ver his

pain; So sad, yet so sweet-ly, he war-bled his

woe, The winds ceased to breathe, and the foun-tains to

flow: Rude winds with com - pas-sion could hear him com-

plain, Yet Chlo-e, less gen-tle, was deaf to his strain.

How happy, he cry'd, my moments once flew!
Ere Chloe's bright charms first flash'd in my view :
These eyes then with pleasure the dawn could survey ;
Nor smiled the fair morning more cheerful than they :
Now scenes of distress please only my sight ;
I 'm tortured in pleasure, and languish in light.

Through changes in vain relief I pursue ;
All, all but conspire my griefs to renew :
From sunshine to zephyrs and shades we repair ;
To sunshine we fly from too piercing an air :
But love's ardent fever burns always the same ;
No winter can cool it, no summer inflame.

But see ! the pale moon all clouded retires ;
The breezes grow cool, not Strephon's desires :
I fly from the dangers of tempest and wind,
Yet nourish the madness that preys on my mind.
Ah wretch ! how can life thus merit thy care,
Since length'ning its moments, but lengthens despair !

SONG XXXIII.

BY WILLIAM HAMILTON OF BANGOUR.

Tune—" Galashiels."

Ah! the [poor] shep - herd's mourn-ful fate, When doom'd to love and doom'd to lan-guish, To bear the scorn - ful fair one's hate, Nor dare dis - close his an - guish. Yet ea - ger looks and dy - ing sighs My se - cret soul dis-co - ver; While rap - ture trembling thro' mine eyes Reveals how much I love her. The ten - der glance, the red'- ning cheek, O'er-spread with ris - ing blush - es, A thou-sand va - rious ways they speak, A thou-sand va - rious wish - es.

For, oh! that form so heavenly fair,
  Those languid eyes so sweetly smiling,
That artless blush, and modest air,
  So fatally beguiling;
Thy every look, and every grace,
  So charm whene'er I view thee,
Till death o'ertake me in the chace,
  Still will my hopes pursue thee.
Then when my tedious hours are past,
  Be this last blessing given,
Low at thy feet to breathe my last,
  And die in sight of heaven.

SONG XXXIV.

UNGRATEFUL NANNY.

BY CHARLES LORD BINNING.*

Did e-ver swain a nymph a - dore, As I un-

grate-ful Nan-ny do? Was e-ver shep-herd's heart so

* Son to the late, and father to the present, Earl of Haddington.
He died at Naples 1732-3, "universally lamented."

sore? Was e-ver bro-ken heart so true? My cheeks are

swell'd with tears, but she Has ne-ver shed a tear for me.

If Nanny call'd, did Robin stay,
    Or linger when she bid me run?
She only had the word to say,
    And all she ask'd was quickly done.
I always thought on her, but she
Would ne'er bestow a thought on me.

To let her cows my clover taste
    Have I not rose by break of day?
When did her heifers ever fast,
    If Robin in his yard had hay?
Though to my fields they welcome were,
I never welcome was to her.

If Nanny ever lost a sheep,
    I cheerfully did give her two:
Did not her lambs in safety sleep
    Within my folds in frost and snow?
Have they not there from cold been free?
But Nanny still is cold to me.

Whene'er I climb'd our orchard trees,
    The ripest fruit was kept for Nan;
Oh how those hands that drown'd her bees
    Were stung! I'll ne'er forget the pain:

Sweet were the combs as sweet could be,
But Nanny ne'er look'd sweet on me.

If Nanny to the well did come,
   'Twas I that did her pitchers fill;
Full as they were I brought them home,
   Her corn I carried to the mill:
My back did bear her sacks, but she
Would never bear the sight of me.

To Nanny's poultry oats I gave,
   I 'm sure they always had the best:
Within this week her pigeons have
   Eat up a peck of peas at least:
Her little pigeons kiss, but she
Would never take a kiss from me:

Must Robin always Nanny woo!
   And Nanny still on Robin frown?
Alas! poor wretch! what shall I do,
   If Nanny does not love me soon?
If no relief to me she 'll bring,
I 'll hang me in her apron-string.

SONG XXXV.

BY WILLIAM HAMILTON OF BANGOUR.

TUNE—"The Yellow-hair'd Laddie." *

YE shepherds and nymphs that adorn the gay plain,
Approach from your sports, and attend to my strain ;
Amongst all your number a lover so true
Was ne'er so undone, with such bliss in his view.

Was ever a nymph so hard-hearted as mine ?
She knows me sincere, and she sees how I pine ;
She does not disdain me, nor frown in her wrath,
But calmly and mildly resigns me to death.

She calls me her friend, but her lover denies :
She smiles when I 'm cheerful, but hears not my
   sighs.
A bosom so flinty, so gentle an air,
Inspires me with hope, and yet bids me despair !

I fall at her feet, and implore her with tears :
Her answer confounds, while her manner endears ;
When softly she tells me to hope no relief,
My trembling lips bless her in spite of my grief.

By night, while I slumber, still haunted with care,
I start up in anguish, and sigh for the fair :
The fair sleeps in peace, may she ever do so !
And only when dreaming imagine my wo.

* Ramsay.   See before, p. 125.

Then gaze at a distance, nor farther aspire ;
Nor think she should love whom she cannot admire :
Hush all thy complaining, and dying her slave,
Commend her to heaven, and thyself to the grave.

SONG XXXVI.*

BY TOBIAS SMOLLETT, M.D.

Thy fa - tal shafts un - err - ing move, I bow before thine al - tar, Love! I feel thy soft, re-
sist - less flame Glide swift thro' all my vi - tal frame

For while I gaze, my bosom glows,
My blood in tides impetuous flows,
Hope, fear, and joy alternate roll,
And floods of transports 'whelm my soul !

My falt'ring tongue attempts in vain
In soothing murmurs to complain,
My tongue some secret magic ties,
My murmurs sink in broken sighs !

* In imitation of a much-admired ode of Sappho's. See Philip's
translation. English Songs, I. 188.

Condemn'd to nurse eternal care,
And ever drop the silent tear,
Unheard I mourn, unknown I sigh,
Unfriended live, unpitied die!

SONG XXXVII.

BY THE REV. ALEXANDER WEBSTER, D.D.

TUNE—" Alloa House." *

The spring-time re - turns, and clothes the green
plains, And Al - lo - a shines more cheer - ful and
gay: The lark tunes his throat, and the neigh - bour-
ing swains Sing mer - ri - ly round me wher - e - ver
I stray: But San - dy nae mair re - turns to
my view: Nae spring - time me cheers, nae mu - sic can

* Composed by Mr Oswald.

charm. He's gane! and, I fear me, for e - ver: a-

dieu! A - dieu ev'-ry plea-sure this bo - som can warm.

O Alloa house! how much art thou changed!
  How silent, how dull to me is each grove!
Alane I here wander where ance we both ranged,
  Alas! where to please me my Sandy ance strove!
Here, Sandy, I heard the tales that you tauld,
  Here list'ned too fond whenever you sang;
Am I grown less fair then, that you are turn'd cauld!
  Or foolish, believed a false, flattering tongue!

So spoke the fair maid, when sorrow's keen pain,
  And shame, her last falt'ring accents suppress'd;
For fate, at that moment, brought back her dear
    swain,
  Who heard, and with rapture, his Nelly address'd:
My Nelly! my fair, I come; O my love!
  Nae pow'r shall thee tear again from my arms,
And Nelly! nae mair thy fond shepherd reprove,
  Who knows thy fair worth, and adores a' thy
    charms.

She heard; and new joy shot through her saft frame,
  And will you, my love! be true? she replied:
And live I to meet my fond shepherd the same!
  Or dream I that Sandy will make me his bride?

O Nelly! I live to find thee still kind ;
  Still true to thy swain, and lovely as true ;
Then, adieu to a' sorrow ; what soul is so blind,
  As not to live happy for ever with you?

SONG XXXVIII.

BY ALLAN·RAMSAY.

Tune—"The Bonnie Lass of Branksome."

As I cam' in by Te - viot side, And by the braes o'
Branksome, There first I saw my bon - nie bride, Young
smil - ing, sweet, and hand-some; Her skin was saft - er than the
down, And white as a - la - bas - ter; Her hair a shin - ing
wav - y brown; In straightness none sur - pass'd her.

Life glow'd upon her lip and cheek,
  Her clear een were surprising,
And beautifully turn'd her neck,
  Her little breasts just rising

Nae silken hose with gushets fine,
  Or shoon wi' glancing laces,
On her bare leg, forbade to shine
  Weel-shapen native graces.

Ae little coat, and bodice white,
  Was sum o' a' her claithing;
Even these o'er mickle;—mair delyte
  She'd given cled wi' naething.
She lean'd upon a flowery brae,
  By which a burnie trotted;
On her I glower'd my saul away,
  While on her sweets I doated.

A thousand beauties of desert
  Before had scarce alarm'd me,
Till this dear artless struck my heart,
  And, bot designing, charm'd me.
Hurried by love, close to my breast
  I clasp'd this fund of blisses;
Wha smiled, and said, Without a priest,
  Sir, hope for nocht but kisses.

I had nae heart to do her harm,
  And yet I couldna want her;
What she demanded, ilka charm
  O' hers pled, I should grant her.
Since Heaven had dealt to me a routh,
  Straight to the kirk I led her;
There " plighted " her my faith and troth,
  And a young lady made her.

M

SONG XXXIX.

THE SILKEN SNOODED LASSIE.

TUNE—" Gala Water."

Com - ing through the broom at e'en, And com - ing through the broom sae drear-y, The las - sie lost her silk - en snood, Which cost her mo - ny a blurt and blear e'e.

Fair her hair, and brent her brow,
    And bonnie blue her een when near ye;
The mair I prie'd her bonnie mou,
    The mair I wish'd her for my dearie.

The broom was lang, the lassie gay,
    And oh but I was unco cheerie;
The snood was tint, a well a day!
    For mirth was turn'd to blurt and blear-e'e.

I press'd her hand, she sigh'd, I woo'd,
    And speir'd, What gars ye sob, my dearie?
Quoth she, I 've lost my silken snood,
    And never mair can look sae cheerie.

I said, Ne'er mind the silken snood,
    Nae langer mourn, nor look sae dreary;
I'll buy you ane that's twice as good,
    If you'll consent to be my dearie.

Quoth she, If you will aye be mine,
    Nae mair the snood shall make me dreary:
I vow'd, I seal'd, and bless the time,
    That in the broom I met my dearie.

SONG XL.

HERE AWA', THERE AWA'.

Plaintive.

Here a - wa', there a - wa', here a - wa', Wil - lie,

Here a - wa', there a - wa', haud a - wa' hame;

Lang have I sought thee, dear have I bought thee,

Now I have got - ten my Wil - lie a - gain.

Thro' the lang muir I have follow'd my Willie,
Thro' the lang muir I have follow'd him hame;
Whatever betide us, nought shall divide us,
Love now rewards all my sorrow and pain.

Here awa', there awa', here awa', Willie,
Here awa', there awa', haud awa', hame ;
Come, love, believe me, nothing can grieve me,
Ilka thing pleases while Willie's at hame.

SONG XLI.

THE MARINER'S WIFE.

BY JEAN ADAMS, CRAWFORD'S-DYKE, GREENOCK.

But are ye sure the news is true? And are ye sure he's
weel? Is this a time to think o' wark? Ye jauds, fling by your
wheel. There 's nae luck a - bout the house, There 's nae luck at a',
There 's nae luck a - bout the house Whan our gude-man 's a - wa' !

Is this a time to think o' wark,
When Colin 's at the door?
Rax me my cloak, I 'll doun the quay,
And see him come ashore.
There 's nae luck, &c.

Rise up, and mak a clean fireside,
   Put on the muckle pat ;
Gie little Kate her cotton goun,
   And Jock his Sunday's coat.
        There 's nae luck, &c.

And mak their shoon as black as slaes,
   Their stockings white as snaw ;
It 's a' to pleasure our gudeman,
   He likes to see them braw.
        There 's nae luck, &c.

There are twa hens into the crib
   Hae fed this month and mair,
Mak haste, and thraw their necks about,
   That Colin weel may fare.
        There 's nae luck, &c.

Bring down to me my bigonet,
   My bishop satin goun,
And then gae tell the bailie's wife
   That Colin 's come to toun.
        There 's nae luck, &c.

My Turkey slippers I 'll put on,
   My stockings pearl blue,
And a' to pleasure our gudeman,
   For he 's baith leel and true.
        There 's nae luck, &c.

Sae sweet his voice, sae smooth his tongue,
　　His breath's like caller air,
His very tread has music in 't,
　　As he comes up the stair,
　　　　There's nae luck, &c.

And will I see his face again?
　　And will I hear him speak?
I 'm dounright dizzy with the joy,
　　In troth I 'm like to greet!
　　　　There's nae luck, &c.

———◆———

SONG XLII.

MY WIFE'S TA'EN THE GEE.

A freen' o' mine cam here yestreen, And he would hae me doun

To drink a pot of ale wi' him, In the neist bur-row's toun.

But oh, in-deed, it was, sir, Sae far the waur for me;

For lang or e'er that I cam hame My wife had ta'en the gee.

We sat sae late, and drank sae stout,
 The truth I tell to you,
'That lang or e'er midnight came,
 We were a' roaring fou.
My wife sits at the fireside,
 And the tear blinds aye her ee ;
The ne'er a bed will she gae to,
 But sit and tak the gee.

In the morning soon, when I cam down,
 The ne'er a word she spake ;
But mony a sad and sour look,
 And aye her head she 'd shake.
My dear, quoth I, what aileth thee,
 To look sae sour on me ?
I 'll never do the like again,
 If you 'll ne'er tak the gee.

When that she heard, she ran, she flang
 Her arms about my neck ;
And twenty kisses in a crack,
 And, poor wee thing, she grat.
If you 'll ne'er do the like again,
 But bide at hame wi' me,
I 'll lay my life I 'se be the wife
 That 's never tak the gee.

SONG XLIII.

THE HAPPY CLOWN.

How hap-py is the ru-ral clown, Who, far re-moved from
noise of town, Con-temns the glo-ry of a crown, And
in his safe re-treat Is pleas-ed with his
low de-gree, Is rich in de-cent po-ver-ty, From
strife, from care, and bus'-ness free, At once both good and great!

No drums disturb his morning sleep,
He fears no danger of the deep,
Nor noisy law, nor courts ne'er heap
    Vexation in his mind :
No trumpets rouse him to the war,
No hopes can bribe, no threats can dare ;
From state intrigues he holds afar,
    And liveth unconfined.

Like those in golden ages born,
He labours gently to adorn
His small paternal fields of corn,
    And on their products feeds :
Each season of the wheeling year,
Industrious he improves with care ;
And still some ripen'd fruits appear,
    So well his toil succeeds.

Now by the silver stream he lies,
And angles with his baits and flies,
And next the sylvan scene he tries,
    His spirit to regale :
Now from the rock or height he views
His fleecy flock, or teeming cows,
Then tunes his reed, or tries his muse,
    That waits his honest call.

Amidst his harmless easy joys,
No care his peace of mind destroys,
Nor does he pass his time in toys
    Beneath his just regard :
He 's fond to feel the zephyr's breeze,
To plant and sned his tender trees ;
And for attending well his bees,
    Enjoys the sweet reward.

The flowery meads, and silent coves,
The scenes of faithful rural loves,
And warbling birds, on blooming groves,
    Afford a wish'd delight :

But, oh ! how pleasant is this life !
Blest with a chaste and virtuous wife,
And children prattling, void of strife,
Around his fire at night !

SONG XLIV.

TWINE WEEL THE PLAIDEN.

Oh, I hae lost my silk-en snood, That tied my hair
sae yel-low; I've gi'en my heart to the lad I lo'ed, He
was a gal-lant fel-low. And twine it weel, my bonnie
doo, And twine it weel the plaid-en; The las-sie lost
her silk-en snood In pu-in' o' the breck-an.

He praised my een sae bonnie blue,
Sae lily white my skin O,
And syne he prie'd my bonnie mou,
And swore it was nae sin O.
    And twine it weel, &c.

But he has left the lass he lo'ed,
　　His own true love forsaken ;
Which gars me sair to greet the snood,
　　I lost among the breckan.
　　　　And twine it weel, &c.

———◆———

SONG XLV.

I 'LL CHEER UP MY HEART.

As I was a walking ae May morning,
　　The fiddlers an' youngsters were making their game ;
And there I saw my faithless lover,
　　And a' my sorrows return'd again.
Well, since he is gane, joy gae wi' him ;
　　It 's ne'er be he shall gar me complain :
I 'll cheer up my heart, and I will get anither ;
　　I 'll never lay a' my love upon ane.

I couldna get sleeping yestreen for weeping,
　　The tears ran down like showers o' rain ;
An' hadna I got greeting my heart wad a broken ;
　　And oh ! but love 's a tormenting pain.
But since he is gane, may joy gae wi' him ;
　　It 's never be he that shall gar me complain :
I 'll cheer up my heart, and I will get anither ;
　　I 'll never lay a' my love upon ane.

When I gaed into my mother's new house,
  I took my wheel and sat down to spin ;
'Twas there I first began my thrift ;
  And a' the wooers came linking in.
It was gear he was seeking, but gear he 'll no get ;
  And it 's never be he that shall gar me complain :
For I 'll cheer up my heart, and I 'll soon get anither ;
  I 'll never lay a' my love upon ane.

SONG XLVI.

MY HEART'S MY AIN.

Tune—" We 'll Kick the World before us."

It's no ver-y lang sin-syne, That I had a lad o' my ain; But now he's a-wa' to an-i-ther, And left me a' my lane. The lass he is court-ing has sil-ler, An' I hae nane at a'; It's nought but the love o' the toch-er That's ta'en my lad-die a-wa'.

But I 'm blythe that my heart 's my ain,
   And I 'll keep it a' my life,
Until that I meet wi' a lad
   Wha has sense to wale a gude wife :
For though I say 't mysel',
   That should no say 't, it 's true,
The lad that gets me for a 'wife,
   He 'll ne'er hae occasion to rue.

I gang aye fu' clean and fu' tosh,
   As a' the neighbours can tell ;
Though I 've seldom a goun on my back,
   But sic as I spin mysel' :
And when I 'm clad in my curtsey,
   I think mysel' as braw
As Susie, wi' a' her pearlin',
   That 's tane my lad awa'.

But I wish they were buckled together,
   And may they live happy for life ;
Though Willie does slight me, and 's left me,
   The chiel he deserves a gude wife.
But, oh ! I 'm blythe that I 've miss'd him,
   As blythe as I weel can be ;
For ane that 's sae keen o' the siller
   Will ne'er agree wi' me.

But as the truth is, I 'm hearty,
   I hate to be scrimpit and scant ;
The wee thing I hae I 'll mak use o 't,
   And no ane about me shall want :

For I 'm a gude guide o' the warld,
   I ken when to haud and to gie ;
For whinging and cringing for siller
   Will ne'er agree wi' me.

Contentment is better than riches,
   An' he wha has that, has enough ;
The master is seldom sae happy
   As Robin that drives the plough.
But if a young lad wou'd cast up,
   To make me his partner for life ;
If the chiel has the sense to be happy,
   He 'll fa' on his feet for a wife.

SONG XLVII.

THE BUSH ABOON TRAQUAIR.

BY ROBERT CRAWFORD.

Hear me, ye nymphs, and ev' - ry swain, I'll
tell how Peg - gy grieves me; Though thus I lan - guish,
thus com - plain, A - las! she ne'er be - lieves me. My

vows and sighs, like si - lent air, Un - heed - ed

ne - ver move her; At the bon - nie bush a-

boon Tra - quair, 'Twas there I first did love her.

That day she smiled, and made me glad,
   No maid seem'd ever kinder;
I thought myself the luckiest lad,
   So sweetly there to find her:
I tried to sooth my am'rous flame,
   In words that I thought tender;
If more there pass'd, I 'm not to blame,
   I meant not to offend her.

Yet now she scornful flees the plain,
   The fields we then frequented;
If e'er we meet she shows disdain,
   She looks as ne'er acquainted.
The bonnie bush bloom'd fair in May,
   Its sweets I 'll aye remember;
But now her frowns make it decay,
   It fades as in December.

Ye rural powers, who hear my strains,
   Why thus should Peggy grieve me?
Oh! make her partner in my pains,
   Then let her smiles relieve me:

If not, my love will turn despair,
My passion no more tender,
I 'll leave the bush aboon Traquair,
To lonely wilds I 'll wander.

———◆———

SONG XLVIII.

BY DR AUSTIN.*

For the lack of gold she's left me, O, And

all that's dear be-reft me, O; She me for - sook for

a great duke, And to end - less woes she's left me, O.

A star and gar - ter have more art Than youth, a

true and faith - ful heart; For emp - ty ti - tles

we must part, And for glit-t'ring show she's left me, O.

* On the marriage of his mistress, Jean, daughter of John Drum-mond, Esq. of Megginch, to James Duke of Atholl, in 17—. This lady, having survived her husband, and married, secondly, Lord Adam Gordon, is still living. The tune is said to be old.

No cruel fair shall e'er more move
My injured heart again to love ;
Through distant climates I must rove,
 Since Jeanie she has left me, O.
Ye powers above, I to your care
Give up my charming lovely fair ;
Your choicest blessings be her share,
 Though she 's for ever left me, O.

SONG XLIX.

WAYWARD WIFE.

BY JANET GRAHAM.

A - las! my son, you lit - tle know The sor - rows
that from wed-lock flow. Fare - well to e - ve - ry day of ease,
When you have got - ten a wife to please. She bide you yet, and
bide you yet, Ye lit-t'e ken what's to be - tide you yet : The half of
that will gane you yet, If a way-ward wife ob - tain you yet.

N

[Your experience is but small,
As yet you 've met with little thrall :]
The black cow on your foot ne'er trod,*
Which gars you sing alang the road.
  Sae bide you yet, &c.

Sometimes the rock, sometimes the reel,
Or some piece of the spinning-wheel,
She will drive at you wi' good will,
And then she 'll send you to the de'il.
  Sae bide you yet, &c.

When I like you was young and free,
I valued not the proudest she ;
Like you I vainly boasted then,
That men alone were born to reign.
  But bide you yet, &c.

Great Hercules and Samson too,
Were stronger men than I or you,
Yet they were baffled by their dears,
And felt the distaff and the shears.
  Sae bide you yet, &c.

---

* This is an ancient proverbial expression. It is used by Sir John
Harrington in his translation of " Orlando Furioso," (b. vi. s. 72,)
where, speaking of some very young damsels, he says,

  "The blacke oxe has not yet trod on their toe."

Again, in Heywoode's " Epigrammes upon Proverbes,"

  " The blacke oxe neuer trode on thy foote."

Query, however, the authenticity of this and the following
stanza. The two lines between brackets are wanting in some
copies.

Stout gates of brass, and well-built walls,
Are proof 'gainst swords and cannon-balls,
But nought is found by sea or land,
That can a wayward wife withstand.
  Sae bide you yet, &c.

SONG L.

GOOD MORROW, FAIR MISTRESS.

Good mor-row, fair mis-tress, the be-gin-ner of strife,

I took ye frae the beg-ging, and made ye my wife:

It was your fair out-side that first took my ee,

But this is the last time my face ye sall see.

Fye on ye, ill woman, the bringer o' shame,
The abuser o' love, the disgrace o' my name ;
The betrayer o' him that so trusted in thee :
But this is the last time my face ye sall see.

To the ground shall be razed these halls and these
    bowers,
Defiled by your lusts and your wanton amours :
I 'll find out a lady of higher degree ;
And this is the last time my face ye sall see.

◆

SONG LI.

BY ALLAN RAMSAY.

TUNE—" Lochaber no more."

Fare-well to Loch-a-ber, and fare-well to my Jean,

Where heartsome with her I've mo-ny a day been: For Loch-

a-ber no more, Loch-a-ber no more. We'll

may-be re-turn to Loch-a-ber no more. These

tears that I shed they are a' for my dear, And

no for the dan - ger at - tend - ing on weir; Tho'

borne on rough seas to a far blood - y shore, May-

be to re - turn to Loch - a - ber no more.

Though hurricanes rise, though rise ev'ry wind,
They'll ne'er make a tempest like that in my mind ;
Though loudest of thunder on loudest waves roar,
That's naething like leaving my love on the shore.
To leave thee behind me, my heart is sair pain'd ;
By ease that's inglorious no fame can be gain'd ;
And beauty and love's the reward of the brave,
And I maun deserve it before I can crave.

Then glory, my Jeanie, maun plead my excuse ;
Since honour commands me, how can I refuse ?
Without it I ne'er can have merit for thee,
And without thy favour I'd better not be.
I gae then, my lass, to win honour and fame ;
And if I should luck to come gloriously hame,
I'll bring a heart to thee with love running o'er.
And then I'll leave thee and Lochaber no more.

SONG LII.

BY SIR GILBERT ELLIOT.

TUNE—"My apron, dearie." *

Plaintive.

My sheep I ne-glect-ed, I lost my sheep-hook,

And all the gay haunts of my youth I for-sook: No

more for A-myn-ta fresh gar-lands I wove, For am-

bi-tion, I said, would soon cure me of love. Oh

what had my youth with am-bi-tion to do? Why

left I A-myn-ta? why broke I my vow? Oh

give me my sheep, and my sheep-hook re-store: I'll

wan-der from love and A-myn-ta no more.

* The original words are preserved in the "Orpheus Caledonius,"
and, with some variation, in the collections of 1769 and 1776.

Through regions remote in vain do I rove,
And bid the wide ocean secure me from love!
O fool! to imagine that aught can subdue
A love so well-founded, a passion so true.

    Oh what had my youth, &c.

Alas! 'tis too late at thy fate to repine;
Poor shepherd, Amynta no more can be thine:
Thy tears are all fruitless, thy wishes are vain,
The moments neglected return not again.

    Oh what had my youth with ambition to do?
    Why left I Amynta? why broke I my vow?
    Oh give me my sheep, and my sheephook
        restore,
    I'll wander from love and Amynta no more.

SONG LIII.

THE HAPPY LOVER'S REFLECTIONS.

BY ALLAN RAMSAY.

Tune—"Alas that I cam o'er the moor."

The last time I came o'er the moor, I left my love be-

hind me: Ye powers! what pains do I en-dure, When

soft i - de - as   mind   me! Soon as   the   rud - dy

morn display'd The beaming day   en - su - ing, I   met   be-

times my   love - ly maid In   fit   re - treats for   woo - ing.

Beneath the cooling shade we lay,
   Gazing and chastely sporting ;
We kiss'd and promised time away,
   Till night spread her black curtain.
I pitied all beneath the skies,
   Ev'n kings, when she was nigh me ;
In raptures I beheld her eyes,
   Which could but ill deny me,

Should I be call'd where cannons roar,
   Where mortal steel may wound me,
Or cast upon some foreign shore,
   Where dangers may surround me,
Yet hopes again to see my love,
   To feast on glowing kisses,
Shall make my cares at distance move,
   In prospect of such blisses.

In all my soul there's not one place
   To let a rival enter :
Since she excels in ev'ry grace,
   In her my love shall centre.

Sooner the seas shall cease to flow,
  Their waves the Alps shall cover,
On Greenland ice shall roses grow,
  Before I cease to love her.

The next time I gang o'er the moor
  She shall a lover find me ;
And that my faith is firm and pure,
  Though I left her behind me :
Then Hymen's sacred bonds shall chain
  My heart to her fair bosom ;
There, while my being does remain,
  My love more fresh shall blossom.

———◆———

SONG LIV.

BY DAVID MALLET.*

Ye woods and ye moun-tains un-known, Be-neath whose pale
sha-dows I stray, To the breast of my charm-er a-lone
These sighs bid sweet e-cho con-vey, Wher-e-ver he

* In " Alfred," a masque.

pen - sive - ly leans, By foun - tain, on hill, or in
grove, His heart will ex - plain what she means,
Who sings both from sor - row and love.

More soft than the nightingale's song,
  Oh waft the sad sound to his ear ;
And say, though divided so long,
  The friend of his bosom is near.
Then tell him what years of delight,
  Then tell him what ages of pain,
I felt while I lived in his sight !
  I feel till I see him again !

———◆———

SONG LV.

THE BROOM OF COWDENKNOWES.

How blythe ilk morn was I to see My swain come o'er
the hill! He skipp'd the burn, and flew to me: I

met him wi' good will. Oh the broom, the bon - nie bon - nie

broom, The broom of the Cow - den-knowes ; I wish I

were wi' my dear swain, Wi' his pipe and my ewes.

I neither wanted ewe nor lamb,
    While his flocks near me lay ;
He gather'd in my sheep at night,
    And cheer'd me a' the day.
        Oh the broom, &c.

He tuned his pipe and reed sae sweet,
    The birds stood list'ning by ;
E'en the dull cattle stood and gazed,
    Charm'd wi' his melody.
        Oh the broom, &c.

While thus we spent our time by turns,
    Betwixt our flocks and play,
I envy'd not the fairest dame,
    Though e'er sae rich and gay.
        Oh the broom, &c.

Hard fate ! that I should banish'd be.
    Gang heavily and mourn,
Because I loved the kindest swain
    That ever yet was born.
        Oh the broom, &c.

He did oblige me every hour,
    Could I but faithfu' be?
He staw my heart : could I refuse
    Whate'er he ask'd o' me?
        Oh the broom, &c.

My doggie and my little kit
    That held my wee soup whey,
My plaidie, broach, and crooked stick.
    May now lie useless by.
        Oh the broom, &c.

Adieu, ye Cowdenknowes, adieu,
    Fareweel a' pleasures there ;
Ye Gods, restore me to my swain,
    It's a' I crave or care.
        Oh the broom, the bonnie bonnie broom,
            The broom of Cowdenknowes :
        I wish I were wi' my dear swain,
            Wi' his pipe and my ewes.*

---

* To this song Ramsay subscribes the letters S. R., the initials,
no doubt, of its author. This, therefore, is certainly not the original, which in Ramsay's own time (as we learn from a duet in
"The Gentle Shepherd") was a popular song. It must, indeed, be
of a much earlier date, as in an old black letter (English) ballad of
Charles or James the Second's time, "To a pleasant Scotch tune,
called 'The Broom of Cowdenknows,'" we find the following
burthen :—

> With oh, the broom, the bonnie broom,
>   The broom of Cowdenknows ;
> Fain would I be in the North Country,
>   To milk my daddie's ewes."

SONG LV.*

"COWDEN"-KNOWES.

BY ROBERT CRAWFORD.

WHEN summer comes, the swains on Tweed
　Sing their successful loves,
Around the ewes and lambkins feed,
　And music fills the groves.

But my loved song is then the broom,
　So fair on Cowden-knowes;
For sure so sweet, so soft a bloom,
　Elsewhere there never grows.

There Colin tuned his oaten reed,
　And won my yielding heart;
No shepherd e'er that dwelt on Tweed,
　Could play with half such art.

He sang of Tay, of Forth, and Clyde,
　The hills and dales all round,
Of Leader-haughs, and Leader-side;
　Oh, how I bless'd the sound!

Yet more delightful is the broom
　So fair on Cowden-knowes;
For sure so fresh, so bright a bloom
　Elsewhere there never grows.

Not Teviot braes, so green and gay,
    May with "this" broom compare,
Not Yarrow banks in flowery May,
    Nor the bush aboon Traquair.

More pleasing far are Cowden-knowes,
    My peaceful happy home,
Where I was wont to milk my ewes
    At e'en amang the broom.

Ye powers that haunt the woods and plains
    Where Tweed with Teviot flows,
Convey me to the best of swains,
    And my loved "Cowden"-knowes.

SONG LVI.

SAE MERRY AS WE HAE BEEN.

A lass that was la-den with care Sat hea-vi-ly un-der a thorn: I lis-ten'd a while for to hear, When thus she be-gan for to mourn: Whene'er my dear shep-herd was there, The birds did me·lo·dious·ly sing, And cold nip·ping win·ter did wear A face that re·sem-bled the spring. Sae mer·ry as we twa hae been, Sae mer·ry as we twa hae been; My heart it is like for to break, When I think on the days we have seen.

Our flocks feeding close by his side,
　　He gently pressing my hand,
I view'd the wide world in its pride,
　　And laugh'd at the pomp of command!
My dear, he would " oft " to me say,
　　What makes you hard-hearted to me?
Oh! why do you thus turn away
　　From him who is dying for thee?
　　　　Sae merry, &c.

But now he is far from my sight,
　　Perhaps a deceiver may prove;
Which makes me lament day and night,
　　That ever I granted my love.

At eve, when the rest of the folk
Were merrily seated to spin,
I set myself under an oak,
And heavily sighed for him.
Sae merry, &c.

SONG LVII.

BY DR JOHN HOADLEY.

Set by Dr GREEN.

Sweet An - nie frae the sea beach came, Where Jock - y

speel'd the ves - sel's side ; Ah, wha can keep their heart at hame,

When Jock - y's toss'd a - boon the tide? Far aff to

dis - tant realms he gargs, Yet I 'll be true as

he has been ; And when ilk lass a - bout him

thrangs, He 'll think on An - nie, his faith - fu' ain.

I met our wealthy laird yestreen,
   Wi' gowd in hand he tempted me,
He praised my brow, my rolling een,
   And made a brag o' what he 'd gie :
What though my Jocky 's far awa',
   Toss'd up and down the awsome main,
I 'll keep my heart anither day,
   Since Jocky may return again.

Nae mair, false Jamie, sing nae mair,
   And fairly cast your pipe away ;
My Jocky wad be troubled sair,
   To see his friend his love betray :
For a' your songs and verse are vain,
   While Jocky's notes do faithfu' flow :
My heart to him shall true remain,
   I 'll keep it for my constant jo.

Blaw saft, ye gales, round Jocky's head,
   And gar your waves be calm and still ;
His hameward sail with breezes speed,
   And dinna a' my pleasure spill :
What though my Jocky 's far away,
   Yet he will braw in siller shine ;
I 'll keep my heart anither day,
   Since Jocky may again be mine.

SONG LVIII.

THE SILLER CROWN.

BY SUSANNA BLAMIRE.

And ye sall walk in silk at - tire, And
sil - ler hae to spare, Gin ye'll con - sent to
be his bride, Nor think o' Don - ald mair. Oh, wha wad
buy a silk - en gown Wi' a poor bro-ken heart? Or
what's to me a sil - ler crown, Gin frac my love I part.

The mind whase every wish is pure,
    Far dearer is to me;
And ere I'm forced to "break" my faith,
    I'll lay me down and dee.
For I hae pledged my virgin troth,
    Brave Donald's fate to share;
And he has gi'en to me his heart,
    Wi' a' its virtues rare.

His gentle manners wan my heart,
    He gratefu' took the gift ;
Could I but think to seek it back,
    It would be waur than theft.
For langest life can ne'er repay
    The love he bears to me ;
And ere I 'm forced to " break " my troth,
    I 'll lay me down and dee.

SONG LVIII.*

THE BONNIE LAD THAT 'S FAR AWA.

Oh how can I be blythe and glad, Or how can I gang brisk and braw, When the bon - nie lad that I loe best Is o'er the hills and far a - wa, When the bon - nie lad that I loe best Is o'er the hills and far a - wa.

* The first verse is old ; the rest are said to be written by Robert Burns.

My father put me frae his door,
    My friends they hae disown'd me a',
But there is ane will tak my part,
    The bonnie lad that's far awa.

A pair o' gloves he bought to me,
    And silken snoods he gae me twa,
And I will wear them for his sake,
    The bonnie lad that's far awa.

O weary winter soon will pass,
    And spring will cleed the birken shaw,
And my young babie will be born,
    And he'll be hame that's far awa.

SONG LIX.

WERENA MY HEART LICHT I WAD DEE.

BY LADY GRISSEL BAILLIE.[*]

There was ance a may, and she lo'ed na men, She big-git her bonnie bower doun in yon glen; But now she cries, Dool! and A well-a-day!
Come doun the green gate, and come here a-way. But now she cries, &c.

[*] Eldest daughter of Patrick first Earl of Marchmont, and wife to George Baillie, Esq. of Jerviswood, whose widow she died on the 6th of December 1746.

When bonnie young Johnnie cam o'er the sea,
He said he saw naething sae lovely as me;
He hecht me baith rings and mony braw things;
And werena my heart licht I wad dee.

     He hecht me, &c.

He had a wee titty that lo'ed na me,
Because I was twice as bonnie as she;
She raised such a pother 'twixt him and his mother,
That werena my heart licht I wad dee.

     She raised, &c.

The day it was set, and the bridal to be,
The wife took a dwam, and lay down to dee;
She maned and she graned out of dolour and pain,
Till he vow'd he never wad see me again.

     She maned, &c.

His kin was for ane of a higher degree,
Said, What had he to do with the like of me!
Albeit I was bonnie, I wasna for Johnnie:
And werena my heart licht I wad dee.

     Albeit I was, &c.

They said, I had neither cow nor calf,
Nor dribbles of drink rins through the draff,
Nor pickles of meal rins through the mill-e'e;
And werena my heart licht I wad dee.

     Nor pickles of, &c.

His titty she was baith wylie and slee,
She spy'd me as I cam o'er the lee ;
And then she ran in and made a loud din,
Believe your ain een, and ye trow na me.
      And then she, &c.

His bonnet stood aye fu' round on his brow ;
His auld ane look'd aye as weel as some's new ;
But now he lets 't wear ony gate it will hing,
And casts himself dowie upon the corn-bing.
      But now he, &c.

And now he gaes " daundring " * about the dykes,
And a' he dow do is to hund the tykes :
The live-lang nicht he ne'er steeks his e'e,
And werena my heart licht I wad dee.
      The live-lang, &c.

Were I young for thee, as I hae been,
We should hae been galloping down on yon green,
And linking it on the lily-white lea ;
And wow gin I were but young for thee !
      And linking, &c.

* So Lord Hailes ; Ramsay and others read " drooping."

SONG LX.

MY DEARIE, AN THOU DEE.

BY ROBERT CRAWFORD.

Love nev-er more shall give me pain, My fan - cy's fix'd on
thee; Nor ev - er maid my heart shall gain, My Peg - gy,
an thou dee. Thy beau - ties did such plea - sure
give, Thy love's so true to me: With - out thee I
shall nev - er live, My dear - ie, an thou dee.

If fate shall tear thee from my breast,
    How shall I lonely stray !
In dreary dreams the night I 'll waste,
    In sighs the silent day.
I ne'er can so much virtue find,
    Nor such perfection see :
Then I 'll renounce all womankind,
    My Peggy, after thee.

No new-blown beauty fires my heart
    With Cupid's raving rage,
But thine, which can such sweets impart,
    Must all the world engage.
'Twas this that, like the morning sun,
    Gave joy and life to me ;
And when its destined day is done,
    With Peggy let me dee.

Ye powers that smile on virtuous love,
    And in such pleasures share,
You who its faithful flames approve,
    With pity view the fair :
Restore my Peggy's wonted charms,
    Those charms so dear to me ;
Oh! never rob me from those arms :
    I'm lost if Peggy dee.

SONG LXI.

THE LOWLANDS OF HOLLAND.

My love has built a bonnie ship, and set her on the sea. With seven-score guid mariners to bear her companie.

There's three - score is sunk, and three-score dead at sea,

And the low-lands of Hol land hae twined my love and me.

My love he built anither ship, and set her on the main,
And nane but twenty mariners for to bring her hame ;
But the weary wind began to rise, and the sea began to
    rout,
My love then and his bonnie ship turn'd withershins
    about.

There shall neither coif come on my head, nor comb
    come in my hair,
There shall neither coal nor candle light shine in my
    bower mair ;
Nor will I love anither ane, until the day I dee ;
For I never loved a love but ane, and he's drown'd in
    the sea.

Oh haud your tongue, my daughter dear, be still and be
    content ;
There are mair lads in Galloway, ye needna sair lament.
Oh ! there is nane in Galloway, there's nane at a' for
    me ;
For I never loved a love but ane, and he's drown'd in
    the sea.

SONG LXII.

AULD ROBIN GRAY.

BY LADY ANN LINDSAY.*

Tune—"The Bridegroom grat."

When the sheep are in the fauld, and the kye at hame, And
a' the warld to sleep are gane; The waes o' my heart fa'
in showers frac my e'e, When my gude-man lies sound by me.

Young Jamie lo'ed me weel, and sought me for his bride,
But saving a crown he had naething beside;
To make that crown a pound, my Jamie ga'ed to sea;
And the crown and the pound were baith for me.

He hadna been awa' a week but only twa,
When my mother she fell sick, and the cow was stoun
　　awa';
My father brak his arm, and my Jamie at the sea,
And auld Robin Gray cam a-courting me.

My father couldna work, and my mother couldna spin,
I toil'd day and night, but their bread I couldna win;
Auld Rob maintain'd them baith, and wi' tears in his ee'
Said, Jenny, for their sakes, O marry me.

* Daughter to the late Earl of Balcarras.

My heart it said nay, I look'd for Jamie back ;
But the wind it blew high, and the ship it was a wreck :
The ship it was a wreck, why didna Jamie dee ?
And why do I live to say wae 's me ?

My father argued sair, though my mother didna speak,
She look'd in my face till my heart was like to break ;
So they gi'ed him my hand, though my heart was in the
    sea,
And auld Robin Gray is gudeman to me.

I hadna been a wife a week but only four,
When mournfu' as I sat on the stane at the door,
I saw my Jamie's wraith, for I couldna think it he,
Till he said, I 'm come back for to marry thee.

Oh sair did we greet, and muckle did we say,
We took but ae kiss, and we tore ourselves away ;
I wish I were dead ! but I 'm no like to dee ;
And why do I live to say wae 's me.

I gang like a ghaist, and I carena to spin ;
I darena think on Jamie, for that would be a sin ;
But I 'll do my best a gude wife to be,
For auld Robin Gray is kind unto me.

Affettuoso.

When the sheep are in the fauld, and the kye at hame, And
a' the [wea - ry] warld to sleep are gane, The waes o' my

heart fa' in showers frae my e'e, When my gudeman lies sound by me.

Andante.

Young Ja - mie lo'ed me weel, and [he] sought me for his bride ; But

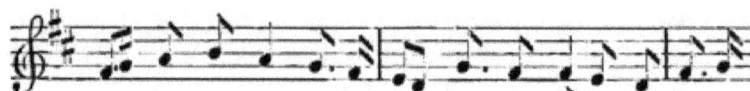

sav - ing a crown he had nae - thing be - side ; To make that

crown a pound my Ja - mie gaed to sea, And the crown and the

pound were baith for me. He had - na been a - wa a

week but on - ly twa, When my mo - ther she fell sick, and the

cow was stoun a - wa'; My fa - ther brak his arm, and my Ja - mie

at the sea, And auld Ro - bin Gray came a - court - ing me.

SONG LXIII.

BY JOSEPH MITCHELL.

TUNE—"Rothes's Lament; or, Pinkie House." *

As Sylvia in a forest lay,
  To vent her woe alone,
Her swain, Sylvander, came that way,
  And heard her dying moan.
Ah! is my love (she said) to you
  So worthless and so vain?
Why is your wonted fondness now
  Converted to disdain?

You vow'd the light should darkness turn,
  Ere you 'd exchange your love;
In shades now may creation mourn,
  Since you unfaithful prove.
Was it for this I credit gave
  To ev'ry oath you swore?
But, ah! it seems they most deceive,
  Who most our charms adore.

'Tis plain your drift was all deceit,
  The practice of mankind:
Alas! I see it, but too late,
  My love had made me blind.

* See before, Song XIV.

For you, delighted I could die :
　　But, oh ! with grief I 'm fill'd,
To think that credulous constant I
　　Should by yourself be kill'd.

This said—all breathless, sick and pale,
　　Her head upon her hand,
She found her vital spirits fail,
　　And senses at a stand.
Sylvander then began to melt :
　　But e'er the word was given,
The heavy hand of death she felt,
　　And sigh'd her soul to heaven.

———◆———

SONG LXIV.

BY DAVID MALLET.[*]

A youth a - dorn'd with ev' - ry art, To warm and win the cold - est heart, In se-cret mine pos-sess'd : The morn-ing bud that fair - est blows, The ver-nal oak that straightest grows, His face and shape ex - press'd, His face and shape ex-press'd.

[*] In " Alfred," a masque.

In moving sounds he told his tale,
Soft as the sighings of the gale
 That wakes the flowery year.
What wonder he could charm with ease !
Whom happy Nature form'd to please,
 Whom Love had made sincere.

At morn he left me—fought, and fell !
The fatal evening heard his knell,
 And saw the tears I shed :
Tears that must ever, ever fall ;
For ah ! no sighs the past recall,
 No cries awake the dead !

SONG LXV.

RARE WILLY DROWN'D IN YARROW.

Wil-ly's rare, and Wil-ly's fair, And Wil-ly's won-drous
bon-nie, And Wil-ly heght to mar-ry me, Gin e'er he
mar-ried ony, [Oh! gin e'er he mar-ried ony.]

Yestreen I made my bed fu' braid,
 This night I 'll make it narrow ;
For a' the live-lang winter night
 I lie twin'd of my marrow.

Oh cam you by yon water-side?
   Pu'd you the rose or lily?
Or cam you by yon meadow green?
   Or saw you my sweet Willy?

She sought him east, she sought him west,
   She sought him braid and narrow;
Syne, in the cleaving of a craig,
   She found him drown'd in Yarrow.

———◆———

SONG LXVI.

BY MISS HOME.

TUNE—"The Flowers of the Forest."*

ADIEU, ye streams that smoothly glide
   Through mazy windings o'er the plain;
I'll in some lonely cave reside,
   And ever mourn my faithful swain.
Flower of the forest was my love,
   Soft as the sighing summer's gale,
Gentle and constant as the dove,
   Blooming as roses in the vale.

Alas! by Tweed my love did stray,
   For me he search'd the banks around;
But, ah! the sad and fatal day,
   My love, the pride of swains, was drown'd.

* See Class IV., Song I.

Now droops the willow o'er the stream,
    Pale stalks his ghost in yonder grove,
Dire fancy paints him in my dream,
    Awake I mourn my hopeless love.

SONG LXVII.

HELEN OF KIRKCONNELL.*

I wish I were where He - len lies, Where day and night she
on me cries, Where day and night she on me cries! I
wish I were where He - len lies, On fair Kirk-con - nell

* The story of this ballad is thus given by Mr Pennant :—

   "In the burying-ground of Kirkconnell is the grave of the fair
Ellen Irvine, and that of her lover : she was daughter of the house
of Kirkconnell, and was beloved by two gentlemen at the same
time ; the one vowed to sacrifice the successful rival to his resent-
ment, and watched an opportunity while the happy pair were sitting
on the banks of the Kirtle, that washes these grounds. Helen per-
ceived the desperate lover on the opposite side, and, fondly thinking to save her favourite, interposed ; and receiving the wound intended for her beloved, fell and expired in his arms. He instantly
revenged her death, then fled into Spain, and served for some time
against the infidels ; on his return he visited the grave of his unfortunate mistress, stretched himself on it, and, expiring on the spot,
was interred by her side. A sword and a cross are engraven on the
tombstone, with *hic jacet Adam Fleming;* the only memorial of

lea! O He - len fair! O He - len chaste! Were I with thee I

would be blest! Were I with thee I would be blest! Where

thou liest low, and at thy rest, On fair Kirk - con - nell lea.

I wish my grave were growing green!
My winding sheet put o'er my een!
I wish my grave were growing green,
         On fair Kirkconnell lea!

Where Helen lies! where Helen lies!
I wish I were where Helen lies!
Soon may I be where Helen lies!
         Who died for luve of me.

this unhappy gentleman, except an ancient ballad of no great merit,
which records the tragical event;" "which," he adds in a note,
"happened either the latter end of the reign of James V. or the
beginning of that of Mary." "Tour in Scotland," II. 101.

The MS. account transmitted to the editor by a learned and ingenious gentleman in Scotland, well known in the literary world,
represents the lovers "walking" instead of "sitting," and takes no
notice of Adam's flight into Spain and service against the infidels,
who were, in fact, completely subdued many years before the reign
of James V. It adds that, "on the spot where Helen fell was
erected a cairn."

Whether this be the "ancient ballad" alluded to by Mr Pennant
is uncertain. Indeed, from the following passage in one written by
"Thomas Poynton, a pauper, after he had read Drummond of
Hawthornden's History of Scotland," printed in the *Gentleman's
Magazine*, for July 1783, there appears some reason to think that it

SONG LXVIII.

THE BRAES OF YARROW.

TO LADY JANE HOME.

IN IMITATION OF THE ANCIENT SCOTISH MANNER.

BY WILLIAM HAMILTON OF BANGOUR.

A. Busk ye, busk ye, my bon - nie bon - nie bride, Busk ye.

busk ye, my win - some mar-row! Busk ye, busk ye, my bon - nie

bon - nie bride, And think nae mair of the Braes of Yar - row.

is not, or at least that the writer describes a very different performance :—

> "T'other day as she work'd at her wheel,
> She sang of fair Eleanor's fate,
> Who fell by stern jealousy's steel,
> As on Kirtle's smooth margin she sate.

> "Her lover, to shield from the dart,
> Most eagerly she interposed;
> The arrow transpierced her fond heart,
> The fair in his arms her eyes closed.

> "O Fleming! how wretched thy doom,
> Thy love to see wounded to death;
> No wonder that, stretch'd on her tomb,
> In grief thou surrend'red'st thy breath.

> "Yet one consolation was thine,
> To soften fate's rigid decree,
> Thy mistress her life did resign,
> A martyr to love and to thee."

B. Where gat ye that bon-nie bon-nie bride? Where gat ye that win-some mar-row? *A.* I gat her where I dare - na weil be seen, Pu - ing the birks on the Braes of Yar - row.

Weep not, weep not, my bonnie bonnie bride,
   Weep not, weep not, my winsome marrow,
Nor let thy heart lament to leive
    Puing the birks on the Braes of Yarrow.

B. Why does she weep, thy bonnie bonnie bride?
   Why does she weep, thy winsome marrow?
And why dare ye nae mair weil be seen
    Puing the birks on the Braes of Yarrow?

A. Lang maun she weep, lang maun she, maun she
       weep,
   Lang maun she weep with dule and sorrow;
And lang maun I nae mair weil be seen
    Puing the birks on the Braes of Yarrow.

For she has tint her luver, luver dear,
   Her luver dear, the cause of sorrow,
And I hae slain the comliest swain
    That e'er pu'd birks on the Braes of Yarrow.

Why runs thy stream, O Yarrow, Yarrow red?
    Why on thy braes heard the voice of sorrow?
And why yon melancholeous weids
    Hung on the bonnie birks of Yarrow.

What's yonder floats on the rueful, rueful flude?
    What's yonder floats?   O dule and sorrow!
'Tis he the comely swain I slew
    Upon the duleful Braes of Yarrow.

Wash, O wash his wounds, his wounds in tears,
    His wounds in tears, with dule and sorrow,
And wrap his limbs in mourning weids,
    And lay him on the Braes of Yarrow.

Then build, then build, ye sisters, sisters sad,
    Ye sisters sad, his tomb with sorrow,
And weep around in waeful wise,
    His hapless fate on the Braes of Yarrow.

Curse ye, curse ye, his useless, useless shield,
    My arm that wrought the deed of sorrow,
The fatal spear that pierced his breast,
    His comely breast on the Braes of Yarrow.

Did I not warn thee not to lu'e,
    And warn from fight? but to my sorrow,
O'er rashly bald, a stronger arm
    Thou met'st, and fell on the Braes of Yarrow.

Sweet smells the birk, green grows, green grows the
    grass,
  Yellow on Yarrow's bank the gowan,
Fair hangs the apple frae the rock,
  Sweet the wave of Yarrow flowan.

Flows Yarrow sweet? as sweet, as sweet flows Tweed,
  As green its grass, its gowan yellow,
As sweet smells on its braes the birk,
  The apple frae the rock as mellow.

Fair was thy luve, fair, fair indeed thy luve,
  In "flowery" bands thou him did'st fetter;
Tho' he was fair and weil beluv'd again,
  Than me, he never lu'ed thee better.

Busk ye, then busk, my bonnie bonnie bride,
  Busk ye, busk ye, my winsome marrow,
Busk ye, and lu'e me on the banks of Tweed,
  And think nae mair on the Braes of Yarrow.

C.   How can I busk a bonnie bonnie bride?
  How can I busk a winsome marrow;
How lu'e him on the banks of Tweed,
  That slew my luve on the Braes of Yarrow?

O Yarrow fields, may never, never rain,
  No dew thy tender blossoms cover,
For there was basely slain my luve,
  My luve, as he had not been a luver.

The boy put on his robes, his robes of green,
   His purple vest, 'twas my awn sewin';
Ah! wretched me! I little, little ken'd
   He was in these to meet his ruin.

The boy took out his milk-white, milk-white steed,
   Unheedful of my dule and sorrow;
But e'er the too-fa' of the night
   He lay a corpse on the Braes of Yarrow.

Much I rejoiced that waeful, waeful day;
   I sang, my voice the woods returning;
But lang e'er night the spear was flown
   That slew my luve, and left me mourning.

What can my barbarous, barbarous father do,
   But with his cruel rage pursue me?
My luver's blood is on thy spear,
   How can'st thou, barbarous man, then woo me?

My happy sisters may be, may be proud,
   With cruel and ungentle scoffin,
May bid me seek on Yarrow Braes
   My luver nailèd in his coffin.

My brother Douglas may upbraid,
   And strive with threatening words to move me,
My luver's blood is on thy spear,
   How can'st thou ever bid me luve thee

Yes, yes, prepare the bed, the bed of luve,
 With bridal sheets my body cover,
Unbar, ye bridal maids, the door,
 Let in the expected husband luver.

But who the expected husband, husband is?
 His hands, methinks, are bathed in slaughter:
Ah me! what ghastly spectre's yon,
 Comes, in his pale shroud, bleeding after?

Pale as he is, here lay him, lay him down,
 O lay his cold head on my pillow;
Take aff, take aff these bridal weids,
 And crown my careful head with willow.

Pale tho' thou art, yet best, yet best beluv'd,
 O could my warmth to life restore thee!
Yet lye all night between my breists,
 No youth lay ever there before thee.

Pale, pale indeed, O lovely, lovely youth,
 Forgive, forgive so foul a slaughter,
And lye all night between my breists,
 No youth shall ever lye there after.

A. Return, return, O mournful, mournful bride,
 Return, and dry thy useless sorrow,
Thy luver heeds nought of thy sighs,
 He lyes a corpse on the Braes of Yarrow.

SONG LXIX.

THE BRAES OF YARROW.*

BY THE REV. JOHN LOGAN,

ONE OF THE MINISTERS OF LEITH.

Thy Braes were bonnie, Yarrow stream !
  When first on them I met my lover ;
Thy Braes how dreary, Yarrow stream !
  When now thy waves his body cover !
For ever now, O Yarrow stream !
  Thou art to me a stream of sorrow ;
For never on thy banks shall I
  Behold my love, the flower of Yarrow.

He promised me a milk-white steed,
  To bear me to his father's bowers ;
He promised me a little page,
  To 'squire me to his father's towers ;
He promised me a wedding ring,—
  The wedding-day was fixed to-morrow ;—
Now he is wedded to his grave,
  Alas, his watery grave, in Yarrow !

Sweet were his words when last we met :
  My passion I as freely told him !
Clasp'd in his arms, I little thought
  That I should never more behold him !

* The air is supposed to be that of the preceding song.

Scarce was he gone, I saw his ghost,
   It vanish'd with a shriek of sorrow;
Thrice did the water-wraith ascend,
   And gave a doleful groan through Yarrow.

His mother from the window look'd
   With all the longing of a mother;
His little sister weeping walk'd
   The green-wood path to meet her brother:
They sought him east, they sought him west,
   They sought him all the forest thorough;
They only saw the cloud of night,
   They only heard the roar of Yarrow!

No longer from thy window look,
   Thou hast no son, thou tender mother!
No longer walk, thou lovely maid!
   Alas, thou hast no more a brother!
No longer seek him east or west,
   And search no more the forest thorough!
For, wandering in the night so dark,
   He fell a lifeless corpse in Yarrow.

The tear shall never leave my cheek,
   No other youth shall be my marrow;
I'll seek thy body in the stream,
   And then with thee I'll sleep in Yarrow.
The tear did never leave her cheek,
   No other youth became her marrow;
She found his body in the stream,
   And now with him she sleeps in Yarrow.

SONG LXX.

WALY, WALY, GIN LOVE BE BONNIE.

Oh wa-ly, wa-ly up the bank, And wa-ly, wa-ly down the brae, And wa-ly, wa-ly yon burn-side, Where I and my love wont to gae. I lean'd my back un-to an aik, I thought it was a trust-y tree, But first it bow'd, and syne it brak, Sae my true love did light-lie me.

O waly, waly, but love be bonnie,
    A little time while it is new,
But when it's auld it waxeth cauld,
    And fades away like the morning dew.
O wherefore should I busk my head?
    Or wherefore should I kame my hair?
For my true love has me forsook,
    And says he'll never love me mair.

Now Arthur Seat* shall be my bed,
   The sheets shall ne'er be press'd by me,
Saint Anton's well shall be my drink,
   Since my true love has forsaken me.
Martinmas wind, when wilt thou blaw,
   And shake the green leaves aff the tree ?
O gentle death, when wilt thou come ?
   For of my life I am wearie.

'Tis not the frost that freezes fell,
   Nor blawing snaw's inclemencie,
'Tis not sic cauld that makes me cry,
   But my love's heart grown cauld to me.
When we came in by Glasgow toun,
   We were a comely sight to see ;
My love was clad in the black velvet,
   And I mysel' in cramasie.

But had I wist, before I kiss'd,
   That love had been so ill to win,
I'd lock'd my heart in a case of gold,
   And pinn'd it with a silver pin.
Oh, oh ! if my young babe were born,
   And set upon the nurse's knee ;
And I mysel' were dead and gane,
   For a maid again I 'll never be !

     * A high hill near Edinburgh.

SONG LXXI.

LADY ANN BOTHWELL'S "LAMENT."

Ba - loo, my boy, lie still and sleep, It grieves me
sore to hear thee weep: If thou'lt be si - lent
I'll be glad, Thy mourn-ing makes my heart full sad.
Ba - loo, my boy, thy mo - ther's joy, Thy fa - ther's
bred me great an - noy. Ba - loo, my boy, lie still
and sleep, It grieves me sore to hear thee weep.

Baloo, my darling, sleep a while,
And when thou "wak'st," then sweetly smile;
But smile not as thy father did,
To cozen maids; nay, God forbid:
But in "thine eye" his look I see,
"The tempting look that ruin'd me."
　　　Baloo, &c.

When he began to court my love,
And with his sugar'd words to move;
His tempting face and flattering cheer
In time to me did not appear;
But now I see that cruel he
Cares neither for his babe nor me.
    Baloo, &c.

I was too credulous at the first
To grant thee "all" a maiden durst;
"Thou swore for ever true to prove,
Thy faith unchanged, unchanged thy love;
But quick as thought the change is wrought,
Thy love's no more, thy promise nought."
    Baloo, &c.

I wish I were a maid again,
From young "men's" flattery I'd refrain;
For now unto my grief I find,
They "all are" faithless and unkind,
Their tempting charms " bred all" my harms,
Witness my babe lies in my arms.
    Baloo, &c.

I take my fate from "bad" to worse,
That I must needs "be now" a nurse,
And lull my young son in my lap;
From me, sweet orphan, take the pap:
Baloo, my boy, thy mother mild
Shall sing, as from all bliss exiled.
    Baloo, &c.

Baloo, my child, weep not for me,
Whose greatest grief's for wronging thee,
Nor pity her deserved smart,
Who can blame none but her " fond" heart ;
For too soon trusting latest " finds"
That fairest tongues have falsest minds.
     Baloo, &c.

Baloo, my boy, thy father's " fled,"
When he the thriftless son has play'd ;
Of vows and oath forgetful, he
Preferr'd the wars to thee and me :
But now, perhaps, thy curse and mine
Makes him eat acorns with the swine.
     Baloo, &c.

Farewell, farewell, thou falsest youth,
That ever kiss'd a woman's mouth ;
Let never any after me
Submit unto thy courtesy ;
For if she do, Oh ! cruel thou
" Wilt" her abuse, and care not how.
     Baloo, &c.

" But curse not him, perhaps now he,
Stung with remorse, is blessing thee : "
Perhaps at death, for who can tell,
Whether the judge of heaven and hell,
" By some proud foe has struck the blow,
And laid the dear deceiver low."
     Baloo, &c.

I wish I were into "the" bounds
Where he lies smother'd in his wounds,
Repeating, as he pants for air,
My name, whom once he call'd his fair:
No woman is so fiercely set,
But "she'll" forgive, though not forget.
    Baloo, &c.

If linen lacks, for my love's sake,
Then quickly to him would I make,
My smock, once for his body meet,
And wrap him in that winding-sheet:
Ay me! how happy had I been,
If he had ne'er been wrapt therein!
    Baloo, &c.

Baloo, my boy, I'll weep for thee,
"Too soon, alake, thou'lt weep for me!"
Thy griefs are growing to a sum,
God grant thee patience when they come!
Born to "sustain" thy mother's shame;
A hapless fate, a bastard's name!
    Baloo, &c.

CLASS THE SECOND.

SONG I.

THE GABERLUNZIE MAN.

BY KING JAMES V.

The pawk-y auld carle came o'er the lea, Wi'
mo-ny gude e'ens and days to me, Say-ing,
Gude-wife, for your cour-te-sie, Will you
lodge a sil-ly puir man? The nicht was
cauld, the carle was wat, And down a-yont the

Q

in - gle   he   sat; My doch - ter's shoul-ders he 'gan

to clap, And cadg - i - ly rant - ed and sang.

O wow! quo' he, were I as free,
As first when I saw this countrie,
How blythe and merry wad I be!
    And I wad never think lang.
He grew canty, and she grew fain;
But little did her auld minny ken
What thir slee twa togither were saying,
    When wooing they were sae thrang.

And O! quo' he, an ye were as black
As e'er the crown of my daddy's hat,
'Tis I wad lay thee by my back,
    And awa' wi' me thou should gang.
And O! quo' she, an I were as white,
As e'er the snaw lay on the dike,
I'd cleed me braw and lady like,
    And awa' with thee I'd gang.

Between the twa was made a plot;
They raise a wee before the cock,
And wilily they shot the lock,
    And fast to the bent are they gane.

Up the morn the auld wife raise,
And at her leisure put on her claise ;
Syne to the servant's bed she gaes,
    To speer for the silly poor man.

She gaed to the bed where the beggar lay,
The strae was cauld, he was away,
She clapt her hands, cried, Waladay,
    For some of our gear will be gane.
Some ran to coffer, and some to kist,
But nought was stown that could be miss'd,
She danced her lane, cried, Praise be blest,
    I have lodged a leal poor man.

Since naething's awa', as we can learn,
The kirn's to kirn, and milk to earn,
Gae butt the house, lass, and wauken my bairn,
    And bid her come quickly ben.
The servant gade where the dochter lay,
The sheets were cauld, she was away,
And fast to the gudewife 'gan say,
    She's aff wi' the gaberlunzie-man.

O fy gar ride, and fy gar rin,
And haste ye find these traytors again ;
For she's be burnt, and he's be slain,
    The wearifu' gaberlunzie-man.
Some rode upo' horse, some ran a fit,
The wife was wud, and out o' her wit :
She couldna gang, nor yet could she sit,
    But aye she cursed and she bann'd.

Meantime far hind out o'er the lea,
Fu' snug in a glen, where nane could see,
The twa, with kindly sport and glee,
　　Cut frae a new cheese a whang :
The priving was good, it pleased them baith,
To lo'e her for aye, he gae her " his" aith ;
Quo' she, To leave thee I will be laith,
　　My winsome gaberlunzie-man.

O kenn'd my minny I were wi' you,
Ill-far'dly wad she crook her mou',
Sic a poor man she 'd never trow,
　　After the gaberlunzie-man.
My dear, quo' he, ye 're yet o'er young,
And haena learn'd the beggars' tongue,
To follow me frae town to town,
　　And carry the gaberlunzie on.

Wi' cauk and keel I 'll win your bread,
And spindles and whorles for them wha need,
Whilk is a gentle trade indeed,
　　To carry the gaberlunzie " on."
I 'll bow my leg, and crook my knee,
And draw a black clout o'er my ee,
A cripple or blind they will ca' me,
　　While we shall be merry and sing.

———◆———

SONG II.

THE JOLLY BEGGAR.

BY KING JAMES V.

There was a jol-ly beg-gar, and a begging he was boun', And he took up his quar-ters in-to a land'art town. And we'll gang nae mair a rov-ing, Sae late in-to the night, And we'll gang nae mair a roving, Let the moon shine e'er so bright, And we'll gang nae mair a rov-ing.

He wad neither lie in barn, nor yet wad he in byre,
But in ahint the ha' door, or else afore the fire.
    And we'll gang nae mair, &c.

The beggar's bed was made at e'en wi' gude clean straw
    and hay,
And in ahint the ha' door, and there the beggar lay.
    And we'll gang nae mair, &c.

Up raise the gudeman's dochter, and for to bar the door,
And there she saw the beggar standin i' the floor.
    And we'll gang nae mair, &c.

He took the lassie in his arms, and to the bed he ran,
O hooly, hooly wi' me, sir, ye 'll wauken our gudeman.
    And we 'll gang nae mair, &c.

The beggar was a cunnin' loon, and ne'er a word he
    spak,
Until he got his turn done, syne he began to crack.
    And we 'll gang nae mair, &c.

Are there ony dogs into this town ? maiden, tell me true,
And what wad ye do wi' them, my hinny and my doo?
    And we 'll gang nae mair, &c.

They 'll rive a' my meal pocks, and do me meikle wrang.
O dool for the doing o't ! are ye the poor man ?
    And we 'll gang nae mair, &c.

Then she took up the meal pocks and flang them o'er
    the wa' ;
The d—l gae wi' the meal pocks, my maidenhead and a'.
    And we 'll gang nae mair, &c.

I took ye for some gentleman, at least the laird o'
    Brodie ;
O dool for the doing o't ! are ye the poor bodie?
    And we 'll gang nae mair, &c.

He took the lassie in his arms, and gae her kisses three,
And four-and-twenty hunder merk to pay the nourice-
    fee.
    And we 'll gang nae mair, &c.

He took a horn frae his side, and blew baith loud and
  shrill,
And four-and-twenty belted knights came skippin' o'er
  the hill.
  And we 'll gang nae mair, &c.

And he took out his little knife, loot a' his duddies fa',
And he was the brawest gentleman that was amang them
  a'.
  And we 'll gang nae mair, &c.

The beggar was a clever loon, and he lap shoulder
  height:
O aye for sicken quarters as I gat yesternight!
  And we 'll gang nae mair, &c.

SONG III.

THE COCK LAIRD.

A cock laird, fu' cadg-ie, With Jen-ny did meet:
He hawsed her, he kiss'd her, And ca'd her his sweet.
Wilt thou gae a-lang wi' me, Jen-ny, Jen-ny?
Thou'se be my ain lem-mane, jo Jen-ny, quoth he.

If I gae alang wi' ye,
    Ye maunna fail
To feast me with caddels,
    And gude hacket-kail.
The deil's in your nicety,
    Jenny, quoth he ;
Mayna bannocks of bear-meal
    Be as gude for thee?

And I maun hae pinners,
    With pearlin's set roun',
A skirt of puady,
    And a waistcoat of broun.
Awa with sic vanities,
    Jenny, quoth he ;
For curches and kirtles
    Are fitter for thee.

My lairdship can yield me
    As meikle a year
As haud us in pottage
    And gude knockit beer ;
But havin' nae tenants,
    O Jenny, Jenny,
To buy ought I ne'er have
    A penny, quoth he.

The borrowstoun merchants
    Will sell ye on tick,
For we maun hae braw things,
    Albeit they soud break :

When broken, frac care
The fools are set free,
When we mak them lairds
In the abbey, quoth she.*

SONG IV.

MY JO JANET.

Sweet sir, for your cour-te - sie, When ye come by the Bass then,

For the love ye bear to me, Buy me a keek-in' glass then.

Keek in - to the draw - well, Jan - et, Jan - et; And

there ye'll see your bon - nie sel', My jo Jan - et.

Keekin' in the draw-well clear,
What if I fa' in, sir?
Syne a' my kin will say and swear,
I droun'd mysel' for sin, sir.

* To "mak them lairds in the abbey" is to compel them to seek
protection within the verge or precinct of Holyrood house, where
debtors are privileged from arrests.

Haud the better by the brae,
  Janet, Janet;
Haud the better by the brae,
  My jo Janet.

Gude sir, for your courtesie,
 Comin' through Aberdeen then,
For the love ye bear to me,
 Buy me a pair of shoon then.
Clout the auld, the new are dear,
  Janet, Janet;
Ae pair may gain ye hauf a year,
  My jo Janet.

But what if dancin' on the green,
 And skippin' like a maukin',
If they should see my clouted shoon,
 Of me they will be taukin'.
Dance ay laigh, and late at e'en,
  Janet, Janet;
Syne a' their faults will no be seen,
  My jo Janet.

Kind sir, for your courtesie,
 When ye gae to the cross then,
For the love ye bear to me,
 Buy me a pacin' horse then.
Pace upon your spinnin'-wheel,
  Janet, Janet;
Pace upon your spinnin'-wheel,
  My jo Janet.

My spinnin'-wheel is auld and stiff,
    The rock o't winna stand, sir,
To keep the temper-pin in tiff,
    Employs richt aft my hand, sir.
Mak the best o't that ye can,
        Janet, Janet ;
But like it never wale a man,
        My jo Janet.

SONG V.

AULD ROB MORRIS.

MITHER.

[There's] Auld Rob Mor-ris, that wons in yon glen,

He's the king o' gude fel-lows and wale o' auld men,

Has four-score o' black sheep, and four-score too:

[And] auld Rob Mor-ris is the man ye maun lo'e.

DOCHTER.

Haud your tongue, mither, and let that abee,
For his eild and my eild can never agree :

They 'll never agree, and that will be seen ;
For he 's fourscore, and I 'm but fifteen.

MITHER.

Haud your tongue, dochter, and lay by your pride,
For he 's be the bridegroom, and ye 's be the bride ;
He shall lie by your side, and kiss ye too :
Auld Rob Morris is the man ye maun lo'e.

DOCHTER.

Auld Rob Morris I ken him fu' weel,
His back it sticks out like ony peet-creel ;
He 's out-shinn'd, in-knee'd, and ringle-ee'd too :
Auld Rob Morris is the man I 'll ne'er lo'e.

MITHER.

Tho' auld Rob Morris be an elderly man,
Yet his auld brass it will buy a new pan ;
Then, dochter, ye shouldna be so ill to shoe,
For auld Rob Morris is the man ye maun lo'e.

DOCHTER.

But auld Rob Morris I never will hae,
His back is sae stiff, and his beard is grown gray :
I had rather dee than live wi' him a year ;
Sae mair of Rob Morris I never will hear.

SONG VI.

NAE DOMINIES FOR ME, LADDIE.

I chanced to meet an air - y blade, A new-made
pul - pit - eer, lad - die, With cock'd-up hat and pow-
der'd wig, Black coat and cuffs fu' clear, lad - die.

A lang cravat at him did wag,
    And buckles at his knees, laddie;
Says he, My heart, by Cupid's dart,
    Is captivate to thee, lassie.

I'll rather chuse to thole grim death;
    So cease and let me be, laddie.
For what? says he. Gude troth, said I,
    Nae dominies for me, laddie.

Ministers' stipends are uncertain rents
    For ladies' conjunct-fee, laddie:
When books and gowns are all cried down,
    Nae dominies for me, laddie.

But for your sake I'll fleece the flock,
    Grow rich as I grow auld, lassie;
If I be spared I'll be a laird,
    And thou's be Madam call'd, lassie.

But what if ye should chance to dee,
    Leave bairnies, ane or twa, laddie?
Naething wad be reserved for them
    But hair-mould books to gnaw, laddie.

At this he angry was, I wat,
    He gloom'd and look'd fu' high, laddie:
When I perceivèd this, in haste
    I left my dominie, laddie.

Fare-ye-weel, my charming maid,
    This lesson learn of me, lassie,
At the next offer hold him fast,
    That first maks love to thee, lassie.

Then I returning hame again,
    And coming doun the toun, laddie,
By my good luck I chanced to meet
    A gentleman dragoon, laddie;

And he took me by baith the hands,
    'Twas help in time of need, laddie:
Fools on ceremonies stand,
    At twa words we agreed, laddie.

He led me to his quarter-house,
    Where we exchanged a word, laddie:
We had nae use for black gowns there,
    We married o'er the sword, laddie

Martial drums are music fine,
    Compared wi' tinkling bells, laddie ;
Gold, red and blue, are more divine
    Than black, the hue of hell, laddie.

Kings, queens, and princes, crave the aid
    Of my brave stout dragoon, laddie ;
While dominies are much employ'd
    'Bout whores and sackcloth-gowns, laddie.

Awa' wi' a' these whining loons,
    They look like Let me be, laddie ;
I 've more delight in roaring guns ;
    Nae dominies for me, laddie.

SONG VII.

SCORNFU' NANCY.

Nancy's to the green-wood gane, To hear the gowd-spink chat-t'ring, And Wil-lie he has fol-low'd her, To gain her love by flat-t'ring : But a' that he could say or do, She geck'd and scorn-ed at him; And aye when he be-

gan to woo, She bade him mind wha 'gat him.

What ails ye at my dad, quoth he,
  My " minny," or my aunty?
With crowdy-mowdy they fed me,
  Lang-kail and ranty-tanty ;
With bannocks of good barley-meal,
  Of thae there was richt plenty ;
With chapped stocks fu' butter'd well ;
  And was not that richt dainty ?

Altho' my father was nae laird,
  ('Tis daffin to be vaunty,)
He keepit aye a gude kail-yard,
  A ha' house and a pantry :
A gude blue bonnet on his head,
  An owrlay 'bout his craigie ;
And aye until the day he died,
  He rade on gude shanks naggie.

Now wae and wonder on your snout,
  Wad ye hae bonnie Nancy?
Wad ye compare yoursel' to me,
  A docken till a tansie?
I hae a wooer o' my ain,
  They ca' him souple Sandy,
And weel I wat his bonnie mou'
  Is sweet like sugar-candy.

Wow, Nancy, what needs a' this din !
   Do I no ken this Sandy ?
I'm sure the chief o' a' his kin
   Was Rab the beggar randy :
His minny Meg upo' her back
   Bare baith him and his billy ;
Will ye compare a nasty pack
   To me your winsome Willy !

My gutcher left a good braid sword,
   Tho' it be auld and rusty,
Yet ye may tak it on my word,
   It is baith stout and trusty ;
And if I can but get it drawn,
   Which will be right uneasy,
I shall lay baith my lugs in pawn,
   That he shall get a heezy.

Then Nancy turn'd her round about,
   And said, Did Sandy hear ye,
Ye wadna miss to get a clout,
   I ken he disna fear ye :
Sae haud your tongue and say nae mair,
   Set somewhere else your fancy ;
For as lang's Sandy's to the fore,
   Ye never shall get Nancy.

SONG VIII.

LASS, GIN YE LO'E ME, TELL ME NOW.

BY JAMES TYTLER.

I hae laid a her-ring in saut, Lass, gin ye loe me, tell me now! I hae brew'd a for-pit o' maut, An' I can-na come il-ka day to woo. I hae a caif will soon be a cow, Lass, gin ye lo'e me, tell me now! I hae a pig will soon be a sow, An' I can-na come il-ka day to woo.

I've a house on yonder muir,
Lass, gin ye lo'e me, tell me now!
Three sparrows may dance upon the floor,
And I canna come ilka day to woo.
I hae a butt, and I hae a ben,
Lass, gin ye lo'e me, tell me now!
I hae three chickens and a fat hen,
And I canna come ony mair to woo.

I've a hen wi' a happity leg,
Lass, gin ye lo'e me, tak' me now!
Which ilka day lays me an egg,
And I canna come ilka day to woo.
I hae a kebbock upon my shelf,
Lass, gin ye lo'e me, tak' me now!
I downa eat it a' mysel;
And I winna come ony mair to woo.*

SONG IX.

FOR THE LOVE OF JEAN.

Jock-y said to Jen-ny, Jen-ny, wilt thou do't? Ne'er a fit,

quo' Jen-ny, for my to-cher gude; For my to-cher gude, I win-na

mar-ry thee. E'en's ye like, quo' Johnnie, ye may let it be.

* There seems to exist an older song with a similar burden; as
Lord Hailes, in his notes on the "Wowing of Jok and Jynny,"
("Ancient Scottish Poems, 1770,") gives the following lines from
"a more modern Scottish ballad:"

"I ha a wie lairdschip down in the Merse,
The nynetenth part of a gusse's gerse,
And I wo'na cum every day to wow."

I hae gowd and gear, I hae land eneuch,
I hae seven gude owsen ganging in a pleugh,
Ganging in a pleugh, and linkin' o'er the lee ;
And gin ye winna tak' me, I can let ye be.

I hae a good ha' house, a barn and a byre,
A stack afore the door, I 'll make a rantin' fire ;
I 'll make a rantin' fire, and merry shall we be :
And gin ye winna tak' me, I can let ye be.

Jenny said to Jocky, gin ye winna tell,
Ye shall be the lad, I 'll be the lass mysel' :
Ye're a bonnie lad, and I 'm a lassie free,
Ye're welcomer to tak' me than to let me be.

SONG X.

BY THE REV. JOHN CLUNIE OF BORTHWICK.

Tune—"Happy Dick Dawson."

I lo'e na a lad-die but ane, He lo'es na
a lass-ie but me ; He's will-ing to mak' me his
ain, An' his ain I'm will-ing to be : He coft me

a roke - ly o' blue, A pair o' mit - tens o'

green, An' his price was a kiss o' my mou;

An' I paid him the debt yes - treen.

My mither's aye makin' a phrase,
    That I 'm lucky young to be wed ;
But lang ere she countit my days,
    O' me she was brought to bed :
Sae mither, just settle your tongue,
    An' dinna be flytin' sae bauld ;
For we can do the thing whan we 're young
    That we canna do weel whan we 're auld.

SONG XI.

HAUD AWA' FRAE ME, DONALD.*

O WILL you hae ta tartan plaid,
    Or will you hae ta ring, mattam ?
Or will you hae ta kiss o' me ?
    And tat 's a pretty ting, mattam.

* See before, Class I., Song XXVIII.

Haud awa', bide awa',
　　Haud awa' frae me, Donald ;
I 'll neither kiss nor hae a ring,
　　Nae tartan plaids for me, Donald.

O see you not her ponnie progues,
　　Her fecket-plaid, plue, creen, mattam ?
Her twa short hose, and her twa spiogs,
　　And a shoulter-pelt apoon, mattam ?
Haud awa', bide awa',
　　Haud awa' frae me, Donald ;
Nae shoulder-belts, nae trinkabouts,
　　Nae tartan hose for me, Donald.

Hur can peshaw a petter hough
　　Tan him who wears ta crown, mattam ;
Hersel' hae pistol and claymore
　　Ta fley ta lallant lown, mattam.
Haud awa', haud awa',
　　Haud awa' frae me, Donald ;
For a' your houghs and warlike arms,
　　You're no a match for me, Donald.

Hursel' hae a short coat pe pocht,
　　No trail my feets at rin, mattam ;
A cutty sark o' goot harn sheet,
　　My motter she be spin, mattam.
Haud awa', haud awa',
　　Haud awa' frae me, Donald ;
Gae hame and hap your naked houghs,
　　And fash nae mair wi' me, Donald.

Ye's ne'er pe pidden work a turn
　At ony kind o' spin, mattam,
But shug your laeno in a scull,
　And tidel highland sing, mattam ;
Haud awa', haud awa',
　Haud awa' frae me, Donald ;
Your jogging sculls and highland sang
　Will sound but harsh wi' me, Donald.

In ta morning when him rise
　Ye's get fresh whey for tea, mattam ;
Sweet milk an ream as much you please,
　Far sheeper tan pohca, mattam.
Haud awa', haud awa,
　Haud awa' frae me, Donald ;
I winna quit my morning's tea ;
　Your whey will ne'er agree, Donald.

Haper Gallic ye's be learn,
　And tat's ta ponny speak, mattam ,
Ye's get a cheese, an butter-kirn,
　Come wi' me kin ye like, mattam.
Haud awa', haud awa',
　Haud awa' frae me, Donald ;
Your Gallic and your highland cheer
　Will ne'er gae down wi' me, Donald.

Fait ye's pe ket a silder protch
　Pe pigger as the moon, mattam ;
Ye's ride in curroch stead o' coach,
　An wow put ye'll pe fine, mattam.

Haud awa', haud awa',
    Haud awa' frae me, Donald ;
For a' your highland rarities,
    You're not a match for me, Donald.

What's tis ta way tat ye'll pe kind
    To a protty man like me, mattam ?
Sae langs claymore pe py my side,
    I'll never marry tee, mattam.
O come awa', run awa',
    O come awa' wi' me, Donald ;
I wadna quit my highland man ;
    Frae Lawlands set me free, Donald.

SONG XII.

THE WOWING OF JOK AND JYNNY.[*]

Robeyns Jok come to wow our Jyn-ny, On our feist-evin
quhen we wer fow ; Scho brank-it fast and maid her bon-nie,
And said, Jok, come ze for to wow ? Scho burn-eist hir baith

* Written before 1568.

breist and brow, And maid her cleir as o - ny clok ; Than spak hir

deme, and said, I trow, Ze come to wow our Jyn - ny, Jok.

Jok said, Forsuth I zern full fane,
  To luk my head, and sit doun by zow.
Then spak hir modir, and said agane,
  My bairne hes tocher gud anewch to ge zow ;
Te he, quoth Jynny, keik, keik, I se zow ;
  Muder, yone man maks zow a mok.
I schro the lyar, full leis me zow,
  I come to wow zour Jynny, quoth Jok.

My berne, scho sayis, hes of hir awin,
  Ane guss, ane gryce, ane cok, ane hen.
Ane calf, ane hog, ane sutbraid fawin,
  Ane kirn, ane pin, that ze weill ken,
Ane pig, ane pot, ane raip thair ben,
  Ane fork, ane flaik, ane reill, ane rok,
Dischis and dublaris nyne or ten :
  Come ze to wow our Jynny, Jok !

Ane blanket, and ane wecht also,
  Ane schule, ane scheit, and ane lang flail,
Ane ark, ane almry, and laidills two,
  Ane milk syth, with ane swyne taill,

Ane rowsty quhittill to scheir the kaill,
    Ane quheill, ane mell the beir to knok,
Ane coig, ane caird wantand ane naill :
    Come ze to wow our Jynny, Jok ?

Ane furme, ane furlet, ane pott, ane pek,
    Ane tub, ane barrow, with ane quheilband,
Ane turs, ane troch, and ane meil-sek,
    Ane spurtill braid, and ane elwand.
Jok tuk Jynny be the hand,
    And cry'd, Ane feist ; and slew ane cok,
And maid a brydell up alland :
    Now haif I gottin zour Jynny, quoth Jok.

Now, deme, I haif zour bairne mareit ;
    Suppois ye mak it nevir sa twche,
I latt zou wit schois nocht miskarrit,
    It is weill kend gud haif I anewch.
Ane crukit gleyd fell our ane huch,
    Ane spaid, ane speit, ane spur, ane sok,
Withouttin oxin I haif a pluche,
    To gang togiddir Jynny and Jok.

I haif ane helter, and eik ane hek,
    Ane cord, ane creill, and als an cradill,
Fyve fidder of raggis to stuff ane jak,
    Ane auld pannell of ane laid sadill,
Ane pepper polk maid of a padell,
    Ane spounge, ane spindall wantand ane nok,
Twa lusty lippis to lik ane laiddill,
    To gang togidder Jynny and Jok.

Ane brechame, and twa brochis fyne,
 Weill buklit with a brydill renze,
Ane sark maid of the Linkome twyne,
 Ane gay grene cloke that will nocht stenze,
And zit for mister I will nocht fenze,
 Fyve hundirth fleis now in a flok ;
Call ze nocht that ane joly menze,
 To gang togidder Jynny and Jok ?

Ane trene truncheour, ane ramehorne sponc,
 Twa buttis of barkit blasnit ledder,
All graith that gains to hobbill schone,
 Ane thrawcruk to twyne ane tedder,
Ane drydill, ane girth, and ane swyne bledder,
 Ane maskene fatt, ane fetterit lok,
Ane scheip weill kepit fra ill wedder,
 To gang togiddir Jynny and Jok.

Tak thair for my parte of the feist ;
 It is weill knawin I am weill bodin ;
Ze may nocht say my parte is leist.
 The wyfe said, Speid, the kaill ar soddin.
And als the laverok is fust and loddin ;
 Quhen ze haif done tak hame the brok.
The rost wes twche, sa wer thay bodin ;
 Syn gaid togiddir Jynny and Jok.

SONG XIII.

MUIRLAND WILLIE.

Heark-en, and I will tell you how, Young Muirland Wil-lie

came to woo; Tho' he could nei-ther say nor do, The

truth I tell to you. But aye he cries, Whate'er be-tide,

Mag-gie I'se hae to be my bride, With a fal, dal, [dal, dal,

dal, de ral, dal, lal, la, ral, lal, la, dal, dal, dal.

On his gray yade as he did ride,
Wi' durk and pistol by his side,
He prick'd her on wi' meikle pride,
    Wi' meikle mirth and glee ;
Out o'er yon moss, out o'er yon muir,
Till he came to her daddy's door,
    With a fal dal, &c.

Gudeman, quoth he, be ye within,
I 'm come your dochter's love to win ;
I carena for making meikle din,
    What answer gi' ye me ?

Now, wooer, quoth he, would ye light down,
I 'll gie ye my dochter's love to win,
    With a fal, dal, &c.

Now, wooer, sin ye are lighted down,
Where do ye win, or in what town?
I think my dochter winna gloom
    On sic a lad as ye.
The wooer he stepp'd up the house,
And wow but he was wond'rous crouse,
    With a fal dal, &c.

I have three owsen in a plough,
Twa good ga'en yads, and gear enough,
The place they ca' it Cadeneugh;
    I scorn to tell a lie:
Besides, I hae frae the great laird
A peat pat, and a lang kail-yard.
    With a fal dal, &c.

The maid put on her kirtle brown,
She was the brawest in a' the town;
I wat on him she did na gloom,
    But blinkit bonnilie.
The lover he stended up in haste,
And gript her hard about the waist,
    With a fal dal, &c.

To win your love, maid, I'm come here,
I 'm young, and hae enough o' gear,
And for mysel' you need na fear,
    Troth try me whan ye like.

He took aff his bonnet, and spat out his chew,
He dighted his gab, and he pri'd her mou',
    With a fal dal, &c.

The maiden blush'd and bing'd fu' law,
She had na will to say him na,
But to her daddy she left it a',
    As they twa could agree.
The lover he ga'e her the tither kiss,
Syne ran to her daddy, and tell'd him this,
    With a fal dal, &c.

Your dochter wad na say me na,
But to yoursel' she has left it a',
As we could gree between us twa ;
    Say what 'll ye gi' me wi' her ?
Now, wooer, quo' he, I hae na meikle,
But sic's I hae ye's get a pickle,
    With a fal dal, &c.

A kilnfu' of corn I 'll gi'e to thee,
Three soums o' sheep, twa good milk kye,
Ye's hae the wadding dinner free ;
    Troth I dow do nae mair.
Content, quo' he, a bargain be 't ;
I 'm far frae hame, make haste, let 's do 't,
    With a fal dal, &c.

The bridal day it came to pass,
With mony a blythsome lad and lass ;
But sicken a day there never was,
    Sic mirth was never seen.

This winsome couple straked hands,
Mess John tied up the marriage bands,
   With a fal dal, &c.

And our bride's maidens were na few,
Wi' tap-knots, lug-knots, a' in blue,
Frae tap to tae they were braw new,
   And blinkit bonnilie ;
Their toys and mutches were sae clean,
They glancèd in our ladses' een,
   With a fal dal, &c.

Sic hirdum, dirdum, and sic din,
Wi' he o'er her, and she o'er him ;
The minstrels they did never blin,
   Wi' meikle mirth and glee.
And aye they bobbit, and aye they beckt,
And ay their wames together met,
   With a fal dal, &c.

SONG XIV.

MAGGIE'S TOCHER.

The meal was dear short syne, We buc-kled us a'
the-gi-ther; And Mag-gie was in her prime, When Wil-lie

made court-ship till her: Twa pis - tols charged by guess, To

gie the court - ing shot; And syne cam ben the lass, Wi'

swats drawn frae the butt. He first speer'd at the guid-man, And

syne at Giles the mi - ther, An ye wad gie's

a bit land, We 'd buc - kle us e'en the - gi - ther.

My daughter ye shall hae,
I 'll gie you her by the hand ;
But I 'll part wi' my wife by my fae,
Or I 'll part wi' my land.
Your tocher it sall be good,
There's nane sall hae its maik,
The lass bound in her snood,
And Crummie who kens her stake :
With an auld beddin' o clacs,
Was left me by my mither,
They're jet black o'er wi' flaes,
Ye may cuddle in them thegither.

Ye speak right weel, gudeman,
But ye maun mend your hand,
And think o' modesty,
Gin ye 'll no quat your land :
We are but young, ye ken,
And now we 're gaun thegither,
A house is but and ben,
And Crummie will want her fother.
The bairns are coming on,
And they 'll cry, O their mither !
We have neither pat nor pan,
But four bare legs thegither.

Your tocher 's be gude enough,
For that you needna fear,
Twa gude stilts to the pleugh,
And ye yoursel' maun steer :
Ye shall hae twa gude pocks
That anes were o' the tweel,
The tane to haud the groats,
The tither to haud the meal :
Wi' an auld kist made of wands,
And that sall be your coffer,
Wi' aiken woody bands,
And that may haud your tocher.

Consider weel, gudeman,
We hae but borrow'd gear,
The horse that I ride on
Is Sandy Wilson's mare :

S

The saddle's nane o' my ain,
An thae's but borrow'd boots ;
And whan that I gae hame,
I maun take to my coots :
The cloak is Geordy Watt's,
That gars me look sae crouse ;
Come fill us a cogue o' swats,
We'll mak na mair toom ruse.

I like you weel, young lad,
For telling me sae plain,
I married when little I had
O' gear that was my ain.
But sin that things are sae,
The bride she maun come furth,
Tho' a' the gear she'll hae,
It'll be but little worth.
A bargain it maun be,
Fy cry on Giles the mither :
Content am I, quo' she,
E'en gar the hissie come hither.
The bride she gade till her bed,
The bridegroom he came till her ;
The fiddler crap in at the fit,
An they cuddl'd it a' thegither.

SONG XV.

WOO'D AND MARRIED AND A'.

Woo'd and mar-ried and a', Mar-ried and woo'd and a',

Was she na ver-y weel aff, Was woo'd and mar-ried and

a'? The bride cam out of the byre, And oh as she

dight-ed her cheeks, Sirs, I'm to be mar-ried the night, And hae

nei-ther blan-kets nor sheets; Hae nei-ther blan-kets nor sheets, Nor

scarce a co-ver-let too The bride that has a' to

bor-row Has e'en right mei-kle a-do. Woo'd and married, &c.

Out spak the bride's father,
 As he cam in frae the plough ;
O haud yer tongue, my dochter,
 And ye's get gear enough ;

The stirk that stands i' the tether,
    And our braw bawsand yade,
Will carry ye hame your corn;
    What wad ye be at, ye jade?
      Woo'd and married, &c.

Out spak the bride's mither;
    What d—l needs a' this pride?
I had nae a plack in my pouch
    That night I was a bride;
My gown was linsy-woolsy,
    And ne'er a sark, ava;
And ye hae ribbons and buskins,
    Mae than ane or twa.
      Woo'd and married, &c.

What's the matter? quo' Willie;
    Tho' we be scant o' claes,
We'll creep the nearer thegither,
    And we'll smoor a' the fleas:
Simmer is coming on,
    And we'll get taits o' woo;
And we'll get a lass o' our ain,
    And she'll spin claes enew.
      Woo'd and married, &c.

Out spak the bride's brither,
    As he cam in wi' the kye;
Poor Willie had ne'er a ta'en ye,
    Had he kent ye as weel as I;

For you're baith proud and saucy,
   And no for a poor man's wife ;
Gin I canna get a better,
   Ise never tak ane i' my life.
     Woo'd and married, &c.

Out spak the bride's sister,
   As she cam in frae the byre ;
O gin I were but married,
   It's a' that I desire :
But we poor folk maun live single,
   And do the best we can ;
I dinna care what I should want,
   If I could but get a man.
     Wood and married, &c.

SONG XVI.

THE BLYTHSOME "BRIDAL."

BY FRANCIS SEMPLE OF BELTREES.

Fy, let us all to the brid-del, For there will be
lilt-ing there; For Jockie's to be mar-ried to Mag-gie, The
lass with the gaud-en hair. And there will be lang-kail and

pot - tage, And ban-nocks of bar - ley meal, And there will be

good salt her - ring, To rel - ish a cog of good ale.

Fy, let us all to the brid-del, For there will be lilt - ing there;

For Jockie's to be married to Maggie, The lass with the gaud - en hair.

And there will be Sandie the sutor,
　　And Willie with the meikle mow;
And there will be Tom the ploutter,
　　And Andrew the tinkler I trow.
And there will be bow-legged Robbie,
　　With thumbless Katie's gudeman;
And there will be blue-checked Dallie,
　　And Lawrie the laird of the land.
　　　　Fy, let us all, &c.

And there will be sow-libber Peatie,
　　And plouckie-faced Wat in the mill,
Capper-nosed Gibbie, and Francie,
　　That wons in the how of the hill;
And there will be Alaster-Dowgal,
　　That splee-fitted Bessie did woo,
And sneevling Lillie, and Tibbie,
　　And Kirstie, that belly-god sow.
　　　　Fy, let us all, &c.

And Crampie that married Stainie,
　　And coft him breeks to his arse,
"Wha after was" hanged for stealing,
　　Great mercy it hapned no warse :
And there will be fairntickled Hew,
　　And Bess with the lily-white leg,
That "gade" to the south for breeding,
　　And bang'd up her wame in Mons-meg.*
　　　　Fy, let us all, &c.

And there will be Geordie McCowrie,
　　And blinking daft Barbra and Mag,
And there will be blencht Gillie-whimple.
　　And pewter-faced flitching Joug :
And there will be happer-arsed Nanzie,
　　And fairy-faced Jeanie be name,
Gleed Katie, and fat-lugged Lizzie,
　　The lass with the gauden wame.
　　　　Fy, let us all, &c.

And there will be girn-again Gibbie.
　　And his glaked wife Jeanie Bell,
And mizlie-chinn'd flyting Geordie,
　　The lad that was skipper himsel'.
There 'll be all the lads and the lasses,
　　Set down in the midst of the Ha',
With sybows, and rysarts, and carlings.
　　That are both sodden and raw.
　　　　Fy, let us all, &c.

* A large old-fashioned cannon, made of iron bars, and capable
of holding two people. It was (for some reason of State, perhaps)

There will be tartan, dragen and brachen,
　　And fouth of good gappocks o' skate,
Pow-sodie, and drammock, and crowdie,
　　And callour nout feet in a plate ;
And there will be partans and buckies,
　　Speldens and haddocks anew,
And sing'd sheep-heads, and a haggize,
　　And scadlips to sup till ye 're fow.
　　　　Fy, let us all, &c.

There will be good lapper'd-milk kebbucks,
　　And sowens, and farles and baps,
With swats, and well-scraped paunches,
　　And brandie in stoups and in caps :
And there will be meal-kail and castocks,
　　And skink to sup till you rive ;
And rosts to rost on a brander
　　Of flouks that was taken alive.
　　　　Fy, let us all, &c.

Scrapt haddocks, wilks, dulse, and tangle,
　　And a mill o' gude sneeshin' to prie ;
Then weary with eating and drinking,
　　We 'll rise up and dance till we die.
　　　　Fy, let us all to the briddel,
　　　　　　For there will be lilting there ;
　　　　For Jockie's to be married to Maggie,
　　　　　　The lass with the gauden hair.

lately removed from Edinburgh to the Tower. [This piece of ord-
nance was sent back to Edinburgh in 1829 at the solicitation of Sir
Walter Scott.—Ed.]

SONG XVII.

JOHNNIE'S GREY BREEKS.

When I was in my se'n-teen year, I was baith blythe and
bon-nie, O; The lads lo'ed me baith far and near, But I lo'ed
nane but John-nie, O. He gain'd my heart in twa three weeks, He
spake sae blythe and kind - ly, O; And I made him new
grey breeks, That fit - ted him most fine-ly, O: He gain'd my heart in
twa three weeks, He spake sae blythe and kindly, O; And I made
him new grey breeks, That fit - ted him most fine - ly, O.

He was a handsome fellow,
    His humour was baith frank and free,
His bonnie locks sae yellow,
    Like gowd they glitter'd in my e'e;

His dimpled chin and rosy cheeks,
    And face so fair and ruddy, O,
And then-a-days his grey breeks
    Were neither auld nor duddy, O.

But now they are threadbare worn,
    They're wider than they wont to be.
They're tash'd-like, and sair torn,
    And clouted sair on ilka knee.
But gin I had a simmer's day,
    As I have had right mony, O,
I'd make a web o' new grey,
    To be breeks to my Johnnie, O.

For he's well wordy o' them,
    And better gin I had to gie,
And I'll tak pains upon them,
    Frae fau'ts I'll strive to keep them free.
To clead him weel shall be my care,
    And please him a' my study, O ;
But he maun wear the auld pair
    A wee, tho' they be duddy, O.

For when the lad was in his prime,
    Like him there werena mony, O ;
He ca'd me aye his bonnie thing,
    "Sae" wha wadna lo'e Johnnie, O ?
So I lo'e Johnnie's grey breeks,
    For a' the care they've gi'en me yet,
And gin we live anither year,
    We'll mak them hale between us yet.

Now to conclude his grey breeks,
  I 'll sing them up wi' mirth and glee ;
Here 's luck to all the grey steeks,
  That show themselves upon the knee :
And if wi' health I'm spared
  A wee while, as I may,
I shall hae them prepared,
  As weel as ony that 's o' grey.

──────◆──────

SONG XVIII.

THE AULD GUDEMAN.

Late in an eve-ning forth I went, A lit-tle be-fore the
sun gaed down, And there I chanced by ac-ci-dent To
light on a bat-tle new be-gun. A man and his
wife were faun in a strife, I can-na weel tell ye
how it be-gan; But aye she wail'd her wretch-ed
life, And cried ev-er, A-lake my auld gude-man.

HE.

Thy auld gudeman that thou tells of,
  The country kens where he was born,
Was but a silly puir vagabond,
  And ilka ane leugh him to scorn
For he did spend, and mak an end
  Of gear that his forefathers wan,
He gart the puir stand frae the door—
  Sae tell nae mair of thy auld gudeman.

SHE.

My heart, alake, is liken to break,
  When I think on my winsome John,
His blinkin' e'e, and gait sae free,
  Was naething like thee, thou dosend drone.
His rosy face, and flaxen hair,
  And a skin as white as ony swan,
Was large and tall, and comely withall,
  And thou 'lt never be like my auld gudeman.

HE.

Why dost thou pleen? I thee maintain,
  For meal and maut thou disna want;
But thy wild bees I canna please,
  Now when our gear gins to grow scant.
Of household stuff thou hast enough,
  Thou wants for neither pot nor pan;
Of siclike ware he left thee bare—
  Sae tell nae mair of thy auld gudeman.

SHE.

Yes, I may tell, and fret mysel',
   To think on these blythe days I had,
When he and I thegither lay
   In arms into a weel-made bed.
But now I sigh, and may be sad,
   Thy courage is cauld, thy colour wan,
Thou faulds thy feet, and fa's asleep,
   And thou 'lt ne'er be like my auld gudeman.

Then coming was the night sae dark,
   And gane was a' the light of day;
The carle was fear'd to miss his mark,
   And therefore wad nae langer stay,
Then up he gat, and he ran his way.
   I trow the wife the day she wan,
And aye the o'erword of the fray
   Was ever, Alake my auld gudeman.

SONG XIX.

TAK YOUR AULD CLOAK ABOUT YOU.*

In winter, when the rain rain'd cauld, And frost and snaw on ilk-a hill, And Bo-reas, wi' his blasts sae bauld, Was threat'ning a' our kye to kill, Then Bell my wife, wha lo'es nae strife, She said to me right hast-i-lie, Get up, gude-man, save Crummie's life, And tak your auld cloak a-bout ye.

* Dr Percy, though he supposes this to be originally a Scotish ballad, has given an ancient copy of it, from his folio MS. in the English idiom, with an additional stanza (the second) never before printed. See the "Reliques of Ancient English Poetry," &c., vol. i. p. 190. The additional stanza is as follows:—

"O Bell, why dost thou flyte and scorne?
  Thou kenst my cloak is very thin:
It is so bare and overworne,
  A cricke he thereon cannot renn:
Then Ile noe longer borrowe nor lend.
  'For once Ile new appareld bee,
To-morrow Ile to towne and spend,'
  For Ile have a new cloake about me."

My Crummie is a usefu' cow,
   And she is come of a gude kin ;
Aft has she wet the bairns' mou,
   And I am laith that she should tyne ;
Get up, gudeman, it is fu' time,
   The sun shines frae the lift sae hie ;
Sloth never made a gracious end,
   Gae tak your auld cloak about ye.

My cloak was anes a gude grey cloak,
   When it was fitting for my wear ;
But now it 's scantly worth a groat,
   For I have worn 't this thretty year ;
Let 's spend the gear that we hae won,
   We little ken the day we 'll die :
Then I 'll be proud, since I have sworn
   To hae a new cloak about me.

In days when our king Robert rang,
   His trews they cost but hauf a croun ;
He said they were a groat o'er dear,
   And ca'd the tailor thief and loon :
He was the king that wore a croun,
   And thou the man of laigh degree,
'Tis pride puts a' the country doun,
   Sae tak thy auld cloak about thee.[*]

---

[*] This stanza, with a little variation, as "king Stephen" for
"king Robert" is sung by Iago, in Shakspeare's tragedy of
Othello, act ii. scene 3.

Ilka land has its ain laigh,*
   Ilk kind of corn it has its hool.
I think the warld is a' gane wrang,
   When ilka wife her man wad rule ;
Do ye not see Rob, Jock, and Hab,
   As they are girded gallantlie, ,
While I sit hurklen in the asse ;
   I 'll hae a new cloak about me.

Gudeman, I wat it's thretty year
   Sin' we did ane anither ken ;
And we have had between us twa,
   Of lads and bonnie lasses ten :
Now they are women grown and men,
   I wish and pray weel may they be ;
And if you prove a gude husband,
   E'en tak your auld cloak about ye.

Bell my wife, she lo'es nae strife ;
   But she wad guide me, if she can,
And to maintain an easy life,
   I aft maun yield, tho' I 'm gudeman.
Nocht 's to be won at woman's hand,
   Unless ye gie her a' the plea ;
Then I 'll leave aff where I began,
   And tak my auld cloak about me.

---

* " Laigh," the undrainable portion of a farm, as useless as the
" hool" is of the corn.—ED.